TOILET TRIVIA

WRITTEN BY MAX BRALLIER
ILLUSTRATED BY JIM STOTEN

LONDON, NEW YORK,
MELBOURNE, MUNICH, and DELHI

Author Max Brallier
Illustrator Jim Stoten
Project Editor Alexander Cox
Project Designer Jess Bentall

Editors Wendy Horobin, Joe Harris,
Ben Morgan, and Lorrie Mack
Designers Gemma Fletcher, Hedi Hunter,
Poppy Joslin, and Lauren Rosier
Production Editor Sean Daly
Production Controller Claire Pearson
Jacket Designer Jess Bentall
Jacket Editor Mariza O'Keeffe
Publishing Manager Bridget Giles
Art Director Rachael Foster
Category Publisher Mary Ling

First published in Great Britain in 2009 by
Dorling Kindersley Limited
80 Strand, London WC2R 0RL

2 4 6 8 10 9 7 5 3 1
TD451 – 07/09

A CIP catalogue record for this book
is available from the British Library.

ISBN 978-1-40534-581-1

Printed and bound by WKT, China

Discover more at
www.dk.com

CONTENTS

CONTENTS

FAMOUS
FIRSTS & LASTS

1ST PLACE — FIRST BIG MAC

In 1968 in Pittsburgh, USA, McDonald's owner Jim Delligatti noticed local Big Boy restaurants selling double-decker burgers. McDonald's HQ let him experiment with the idea and soon he had two burgers, cheese, pickles, onions, lettuce, and special sauce – the world's first Big Mac!

FIRST BOTTLE OF COCA-COLA

1ST PLACE

Invented by pharmacist John Pemberton, the first bottle of Coca-Cola was sold on 8th May 1886 at Jacob's Pharmacy in Atlanta, USA.

FIRST TRANSATLANTIC SOLO FLIGHT BY A WOMAN

1ST PLACE

In 1932, Amelia Earhart became the first woman to fly solo across the Atlantic Ocean. It took her 15 hours.

LAST QUEEN OF FRANCE

LAST PLACE

Maria Antonia Josefa Joanna von Habsburg-Lothringen, better known as Marie Antoinette, was the last queen of France. In 1793, during the French Revolution, she was tried for treason and executed by guillotine. She was 37 years old.

FIRST MICKEY MOUSE CARTOON

Steamboat Willie, featuring everyone's favourite cartoon mouse as a steamboat captain, was released on 18th November 1928.

LAST CONCORDE FLIGHT

The supersonic Concorde airliner made its last flight, from New York to London, on 24th October 2003.

FIRST MAN ON THE MOON

On 21st July 1969, American astronaut Neil Armstrong became the first person to set foot on the Moon. He made the famous statement, "That's one small step for man, one giant leap for mankind."

LAST DODO BIRD

The dodo was a flightless, goofy-looking pigeon that lived on the island of Mauritius, off the coast of Africa. The last dodo died in 1681.

LAST BEATLES CONCERT

The last time John, Paul, George, and Ringo all performed together on stage was 29th August 1966 at Candlestick Park in San Francisco, USA. The stadium was just about half full – imagine the crowd if people had known it was to be their last concert!

FIRST ITEM SOLD ON EBAY

The first item auctioned on eBay was sold by the company's founder, Pierre Omidyar, 1995. He auctioned off a broken laser pointer for $14.

ALL ABOUT DINOSAURS

FAST RUNNER
Velociraptor means "swift thief".

MR NASTY
Tyrannosaurus rex is the most famous of all the dinosaurs. The name means "tyrant lizard king" – so you know he was tough. The average tyrannosaur was 12 m (40 ft) long, 6 m (20 ft) tall, and weighed about 6.5 tonnes (8 tons).

HORN FACE
The *Triceratops* is instantly recognizable because of its short nasal horn and the two big horns on top of its head. The name *Triceratops* means "three-horned face".

Scientists think the *Bruhathkayosaurus* was the biggest of all the dinosaurs. They estimate it was 43 m (140 ft) long and weighed 180 tonnes (225 tons).

NOT SO SCARY
The smallest dinosaur was the *Compsognathus* – it was about the size of a chicken!

SPACE DINOSAURS?
Yes, there are dinosaurs in space – although we're the ones who put them there. In 1998, a fossil *Coelophysis* skull was taken to the Mir space station on the space shuttle *Endeavour*.

Dinosaurs were reptiles that lived between 220 million and 65 million years ago, during the Triassic, Jurassic, and Cretaceous periods of geological time. In movies and on TV you usually just see the big, crazy-looking ones. But there were all sorts of dinosaurs – big ones, small ones, herbivores (plant eaters), and carnivores (meat eaters).

SCARIEST DINOSAUR

Most people think the *Velociraptor* was the most dangerous of the dinosaurs, but that's not true – the *Utahraptor* was even worse. It was one of the most vicious and lethal killing machines that ever walked on Earth. It was larger than the *Velociraptor* and had even bigger claws.

It's one of the biggest questions in science – what caused the extinction of the dinosaurs? Well, no one knows for sure, but scientists suspect that a giant asteroid crashed into Earth and kicked up so much dust and dirt into the atmosphere that it blocked the sunlight and the climate changed. Dinosaurs couldn't handle the changes, and eventually died out.

SMARTY PANTS

In comparison to its relatively small body size, the *Troodon* had the biggest brain of any dinosaur.

FALSE OR FALSE?

YOU CAN SEE THE GREAT WALL OF CHINA FROM SPACE

False. You can't see the Great Wall because it's too narrow, but you can see the pyramids at Giza in Egypt, and the Hoover dam in the USA.

SWEAT SMELLS BAD

False. Sweat has no odour. It's the bacteria that live and thrive on the sweat that smell bad. Soap and water get rid of the bacteria, so don't forget those armpits!

"FALSE OR FALSE?"

BULLS GET ANGRY AT THE COLOUR RED

False. Actually, bulls are colour-blind. As far as they're concerned, you could be waving a nice blue tartan at them.

"FALSE OR FALSE?"

HOLLYWOOD IS TOPS FOR FILM NUMBERS

False. India produces three times as many movies as Hollywood every year.

CATS ALWAYS LAND ON THEIR FEET

False. It's true that cats have a great sense of balance, but they can be badly injured in falls from any height. So – NO – you can't drop your neighbour's cat off the roof.

GEORGE WASHINGTON HAD WOODEN TEETH

False. George had the best teeth available in those days, crafted from walrus ivory.

"FALSE OR FALSE?"

PEOPLE WHO WON'T LOOK YOU IN THE EYE WHEN THEY TALK ARE UNTRUSTWORTHY

False. Psychologists have discovered that con artists and habitual liars are more likely to maintain steady eye contact than any other group of people.

THE WORLD'S MOST EXPENSIVE COFFEE IS EXCRETED BY A WEASEL

False. It's actually an animal called a civet. Coffee beans have a fleshy outer layer, like a cherry, that civets love to eat. They digest the fruit, but the beans pass through their gut. The droppings are collected and the beans are washed before being roast and ground. Mmm... smell that coffee!

CREATURES

FROM THE DEEP

JOKES!
Q: Why are fish so clever?
A: Because they live in schools!

Q: Why is it so easy to weigh fish?
A: They have their own scales!

The **BLUE WHALE** is the largest animal on Earth. It weighs up to 170 tonnes (187 tons) – as much as 2500 people – and can reach 33 m (108 ft) long. The **HEART** of a blue whale is about the size of a Volkswagen Beetle.

THE WHISTLE of the blue whale is the loudest sound produced by any animal on Earth. Lucky they don't live next door!

The **GIANT PACIFIC OCTOPUS** is the largest octopus in the world. The biggest one ever caught weighed 272 kg (600 lb) and had tentacles 9 m (30 ft) long.

GOLDFISH can live for decades if you look after them well. The oldest known pet goldfish, "Goldie", lived to be 45. Most live only 5–10 years.

An OCTOPUS has 3 hearts.

FLYING FISH don't truly fly – they glide over the waves, using wing-like fins to catch updrafts. The longest recorded glide lasted 45 seconds.

In **JAPAN** electric eels have been used to power **CHRISTMAS** trees.

There are more than **25,000 IDENTIFIED** species of fish in Earth's oceans, and scientists estimate there might be another **15,000 SPECIES** still to be found.

A baby fish is called a **FRY**.

The **SMALLEST FISH** is the Philippine goby. It's less than 0.8 cm (⅓ in) long when fully grown.

SHARKS are the most feared of the underwater creatures, but they kill only about 10 people a year. Deer kill about 100 people a year, and coconuts kill about 150. So relax about the sharks... **BUT FEAR THE COCONUT!**

Starfish have **EIGHT EYES** – one at the end of each tentacle. But no brain or heart!

SEA HORSES tend to mate under a full moon. How romantic! After mating, males carry the eggs and eventually give birth.

15

CRAZY COINCIDENCES

LIFE IS FULL OF LITTLE QUIRKS AND COINCIDENCES! BUT SOME ARE JUST INCREDIBLE AND QUITE FRANKLY BIZARRE!

"THE MOST ASTONISHINGLY INCREDIBLE COINCIDENCE IMAGINABLE WOULD BE THE COMPLETE ABSENCE OF ALL COINCIDENCES."
John Allen Paulos
Mathematician

SHIPWRECKED

IN 1885, PLAYWRIGHT ARTHUR LAW WROTE *CAROLINE*, A PLAY ABOUT A MAN NAMED ROBERT GOLDING, THE SOLE SURVIVOR OF A SHIPWRECK. JUST DAYS AFTER THE PLAY'S OPENING NIGHT, A SHIP NAMED THE *CAROLINE* SANK AND ONE MAN SURVIVED - A ROBERT GOLDING.

Lightning strikes thrice!

In 1899, a man in Taranto, Italy, was standing in his garden when he was struck and killed by a bolt of lightning. Thirty years later, his son was killed in the exact same spot – again, by a bolt of lightning. Then, in 1949, Rolla Primarda, the grandson of the first man and the son of the second, was struck and killed by a bolt of lightning in the exact same spot.

Just lying around...

In 1973, actor Anthony Hopkins was to appear in an adaptation of the book *The Girl From Petrovka* – but couldn't find a copy of the book anywhere. He then found one lying on a bench at a train station. It turned out to be the author's own copy that he had lent to a friend, who had lost it!

CRAZY!

LUCKY KID

A man named Joseph Figlock was walking down a Detroit street in the 1930s when a baby fell from a window. Luckily, Figlock broke the baby's fall and they were both unharmed. Then, a year later, the exact same baby fell – and landed on Joseph Figlock! Again, they were both unharmed.

17

BIGGEST...

Too fast to catch, too slow to notice, too big to handle, or too small to see? Here's a list of all these things and more...

Biggest Burrito – In 1997, Californian restaurants joined together to create the world's largest burrito. When finished it measured 1,090 m (3,578 ft) long and weighed the same as a White Rhinoceros – 2,021 kg (4,456 lb). Hope they were hungry.

Biggest Book – *Bhutan: A Visual Odyssey Across the Last Himalayan Kingdom* by Michael Halley is nearly the size of a table tennis table and weighs more than 60 kg (130 lb)!

FASTEST
SLOWEST

Fastest Production Car – Bugatti Veyron. With 1001-brake-horsepower this expensive car (£850,000) can go from 0-60 mph in 2.46 seconds. And has a hair-messing top speed of 407 km/h (253 mph)!

Slowest Animal – Not counting sea creatures like sponges, which don't move at all (lazy layabouts), the slowest animal in the world is the sloth.

SMALLEST

Biggest Man-Made Structure – For centuries, the biggest man-made structure on Earth was the Great Wall of China. But today, it's the Fresh Kills landfill in New York, USA. At its peak, it towered a staggering 23 m (75 ft) taller than the Statue of Liberty. That's a LOT of rubbish.

Biggest Baby – She ain't heavy she's my sister. Nadia Khalina of Siberia was born weighing more than 7 kg (17 lb), making her the world's heaviest baby.

Smallest Sculptures – Artist Willard Wigan creates some of the smallest sculptures on Earth. He works on rice or grains of sand and uses a surgical blade to sculpt tiny creations. If you thought dwarves were small check out Snow White and her friends above – inside the eye of a needle!

Fastest Roller Coaster

The fastest roller coaster in the world is Kinga Ka at Six Flags Great Adventure in USA. At its fastest dip it can hit speeds of 206 km/h (128 mph).

Fastest Bird – The peregrine falcon is the fastest bird in the sky and the fastest living creature alive. When flying, it reaches speeds of 200 km/h (125 mph). When it dives, it can glide close to 275 km/h (170 mph)!

Fastest Animal on Land – The cheetah. It can sprint at speeds of up to 96 km/h (60 mph).

WOULD YOU RATHER?

Homework or video games? Beefburger or cabbage? Some choices in life are easy… others require a bit of a think.

Be a genius **or** be a millionaire.

Get paper cuts whenever you pick up paper **or** be allergic to the rain and turn bright red whenever you get wet.

Spend the rest of your life in jail, surrounded by criminals **or** spend the rest of your life in the woods, alone.

Always be really, really sweaty **or** always be really, really thirsty.

Burp fire **or** fart lightning.

Eat a gigantic spider **or** wrestle 30 rats.

Discover your next-door neighbours are vampires **or** find out your teacher is an alien.

Live in the zoo **or** live in a museum.

Walk across hot coals **or** swim across an icy river.

Be able to fly **or** be invisible.

Never have homework again **or** only have school three days a week.

Go a year without television **or** go a year without dessert.

Go a whole week without talking **or** go a whole year without fizzy drinks.

Live in a world where the Sun never sets **or** live in a world where it's always dark.

Be lost in the middle of a really, really big city **or** be trapped in a really, really small cupboard.

Be really, really short **or** be really, really tall.

Never be able to eat your favourite food again **or** have to eat your least-favourite food five times a week.

Make a tonne of money doing something you hate **or** make less money doing something you love.

Smell of fish all the time **or** have a tail like a monkey.

BEST THINGS EVER SAID ABOUT SPORTS

"I wanted to have **A CAREER IN SPORTS** when I was young, but I had to give it up. I'm only six feet tall, so I couldn't play basketball. I'm only 190 pounds, so I couldn't play football. And I have 20–20 vision, so I couldn't be a referee."

JAY LENO
TALK-SHOW HOST

"There's more to **BOXING** than hitting. There's not getting hit, for instance."

GEORGE FOREMAN
BOXER

"**AWARDS** become corroded, friends gather no dust."

JESSE OWENS
ATHLETE

"**WINNING** is everything. The only ones who remember you when you come second are your wife and your dog."

DAMON HILL
RACING DRIVER

"I've missed more than 9000 shots in my career. I've lost almost 300 games. 26 times, I've been trusted to take the game winning shot and missed. I've failed over and over and over again in my life. And **THAT IS WHY I SUCCEED**."

MICHAEL JORDAN
BASKETBALL PLAYER

"SUCCESS **IS NO** ACCIDENT. It is hard work, perseverance, learning, studying, sacrifice and most of all, love of what you are doing or learning to do."
PELE
FOOTBALL LEGEND

"Whoever said, 'It's not whether you **WIN OR LOSE** that counts,' probably lost."
MARTINA NAVRATILOVA,
TENNIS STAR

"All good athletes make **MISTAKES**; the great ones learn to make that mistake only once."
RAUL LOPEZ
BASKETBALL PLAYER

"Some people think football is a **MATTER OF LIFE AND DEATH.** I don't like that attitude. I can assure them it is much more serious than that."
BILL SHANKLY
MANAGER,
LIVERPOOL F.C.
1959-74

"It's just a job. Grass grows, birds fly, waves pound the sand. **I BEAT PEOPLE UP.**"
MUHAMMAD ALI
BOXER

"Doctors and scientists said that breaking the four-minute mile was **IMPOSSIBLE**, that one would die in the attempt. Thus, when I got up from the track after collapsing at the finish line, I figured I was dead."
ROGER BANNISTER
ATHLETE

23

WHO AM I?

Can you figure out who I am, where I am, and what I am? Here are some clues – each one is a little easier than the last. If you're stumped, the answers are on p.126.

1 I WAS BORN IN 1901.

2 I HAD A BROTHER NAMED ROY.

3 I ONCE SAID "ALL OUR DREAMS CAN COME TRUE, IF WE HAVE THE COURAGE TO PURSUE THEM".

WHERE AM I?

1 I can be seen in dozens of movies, TV shows, and video games.

2 I was originally supposed to last only 20 years – but people liked me so much, they decided to let me stick around!

3 Construction on me finished in 1889.

4 I've been visited by more than 200 million people.

WHAT AM I?

3 I AM MECHANICAL

1 NO ONE PERSON INVENTED ME – THOUGH I CAME ABOUT IN THE 18TH CENTURY.

2 ORIGINALLY, I WAS DESIGNED FOR USE BY THE BLIND.

4 I HAVE A STAR ON THE HOLLYWOOD WALK OF FAME.

5 I RECEIVED 59 ACADEMY-AWARD NOMINATIONS AND WON 26 OSCARS – THOSE ARE RECORDS!

6 I GAVE MY NAME TO ONE OF THE BIGGEST COMPANIES IN THE WORLD.

7 I HAVE MY OWN WORLD AND MY OWN LAND.

8 WHEN YOU THINK OF ANIMATED MOVIES, YOU PROBABLY THINK OF ME.

9 MY FAMILY NAME WAS ORIGINALLY SPELLED D'ISIGNY.

10 I CO-CREATED MICKEY MOUSE.

5 I'm 324 m (1,063 ft) high.

8 I'm built out of 8,565 tonnes (9,441 tons) of wrought iron.

6 From the ground to the top, I have 1,710 steps.

9 I'm in Paris, France.

7 When I was first built, I was the tallest structure in the world.

6 I was designed by the engineer Gustave Eiffel.

4 I PIONEERED THE WORD "QWERTY".

5 I HAVE OVER 40 KEYS, BUT NO LOCKS.

6 MY SOUND IS USED AS PERCUSSION ON THE DOLLY PARTON SONG, "9 TO 5".

7 I LED TO OTHER INVENTIONS, INCLUDING TIPP-EX.

8 PART OF MY NAME FORMS A VERB IN USE TODAY.

9 WHY USE A PEN AND PAPER?

10 I HAVE BEEN MADE REDUNDANT BY THE DEVELOPMENT OF THE COMPUTER WORD PROCESSOR.

CHICHEN ITZA

BUILT: About 600 CE
WHERE: Mexico
WHY? This amazing ruined city in the Mexican jungle was built by the lost Mayan civilization. Its centrepiece is a spectacular stone pyramid.

CHRIST THE REDEEMER

BUILT: 1931 CE
WHERE: Rio de Janeiro, Brazil
WHY? This gigantic concrete statue of Jesus Christ stands on the peak of Corcovado Mountain, overlooking the city of Rio de Janeiro. It's 38 m (120 ft) tall and 635 tonnes (700 tons) in weight.

7 NEW

TAJ MAHAL

BUILT: About 1648 CE
WHERE: Agra, India
WHY? Emperor Shah Jahan, ruler of India's Mughal Empire, built this mausoleum in memory of his favourite wife, who died giving birth.

MACHU PICCHU

BUILT: About 1450 CE
WHERE: Peru
WHY? The "lost city of the Incas" is perched so high in the Andes Mountains that it is usually hidden in the clouds.

ROMAN COLOSSEUM

BUILT: 80 CE
WHERE: Rome, Italy
WHY? The great amphitheatre sat in the centre of the city. Over 500,000 gladiators fought and died in games held to entertain the Roman citizens.

GREAT WALL OF CHINA

BUILT: 500 BCE – 1500 CE
WHERE: China
WHY? Built to protect China's northern borders, the wall once stretched for 8,852 km (5,500 miles), including its many branches. Contrary to popular belief, it isn't visible from space.

WONDERS OF THE WORLD

PETRA

BUILT: About 100 BCE
WHERE: Jordan
WHY? Hidden between towering walls of rock in the Jordanian mountains are the ruins of an ancient desert kingdom. Its most majestic building, as decorative as a Greek temple, was carved out of a sheer cliff. It was a secret to the Western world until Swiss explorers found it in 1812.

CAN YOU NAME THE SEVEN WONDERS OF THE ANCIENT WORLD?
Answers on page 126

BRAINTEASERS

Feeling a little sluggish? Here are some mental puzzles to tease your brain – answers on p.126.

1

HOW MANY TOYS CAN YOU FIT IN AN EMPTY BOX?

2

A man is trapped on an island, surrounded by water. He can't swim. Then, suddenly, one day he escapes. He uses no tools. **HOW DID HE DO IT?**

3

Two women play five games of draughts. Each woman wins the same number of games. There are no ties. **HOW IS THIS POSSIBLE?**

7 Two fathers and two sons went out to eat. Everyone ate one burger, but only three burgers were eaten in all. **HOW CAN THIS BE?**

6 HOW MANY SECONDS ARE THERE IN A YEAR?

5 What **FIVE-LETTER WORD** becomes shorter when you add two letters to it?

4 A man was taking a walk down the street when it began to rain. He wasn't wearing a hat and he didn't have an umbrella, yet somehow, he got home without wet hair. **HOW DID HE DO IT?**

WEIRD NUMBERS

All those maths teachers were right – the world **IS** full of numbers, and here are a few **AMAZING NUMBERS** that can do amazing things.

The Pirahã tribe in the Amazon only count to two – all numbers above that are "many".

FORWARDS AND BACKWARDS
$$111,111,111 \times 111,111,111 = 12,345,678,987,654,321$$

WATCH FOR 47s!

A group known as the 47 society believes that the number 47 is the ultimate random number – they believe that it appears throughout the world more often than any other number. Try it out – keep your eyes peeled for the number 47. Do you think it appears more often than other numbers?

PRIME TIME

Prime numbers can only be divided by themselves or 1. The prime number 73,939,133 is a very interesting prime number – no matter how many digits you chop off the end, you still end up with a prime number. It's the largest prime known to have this property.

NUMBER WEIRDNESS

$$1 \times 8 + 1 = 9$$
$$12 \times 8 + 2 = 98$$
$$123 \times 8 + 3 = 987$$
$$1,234 \times 8 + 4 = 9,876$$
$$12,345 \times 8 + 5 = 98,765$$
$$123,456 \times 8 + 6 = 987,654$$
$$1,234,567 \times 8 + 7 = 9,876,543$$
$$12,345,678 \times 8 + 8 = 98,765,432$$
$$123,456,789 \times 8 + 9 = 987,654,321$$

UNLUCKY 13

Triskaidekaphobia is the fear of the number 13. In 1881, a group of New Yorkers formed the Thirteen Club, determined to end their phobia. On Friday the 13th, at 8:13 p.m., 13 of them sat down for dinner in room 13. Nothing happened.

ALL ABOUT PI

Pi is the ratio of the circumference of a circle to its diameter. It's always the same number, whatever the size of the circle. Pi is pretty amazing because it's a never-ending number. It's usually written as 3.14, but it can get much more precise than that. For example:
$3.1415926535897932384б7$, and on and on and on. The symbol for pi (the Greek letter "p") was first introduced by the English mathematician William Jones in 1706, who stated that $\pi = 3.14159$. This is now the standard symbol for pi.

CALCULATOR MAGIC

- Take the day of the month on which you were born.
- Multiply it by 4.
- Add 13.
- Multiply by 25.
- Subtract 200.
- Add the number of the month you were born.
- Multiply by 2.
- Subtract 40.
- Multiply by 50.
- Add the last two digits of the year in which you were born.
- Subtract 10,500.

WHAT DO YOU GET?
RECOGNIZE THAT NUMBER?
WEIRD, OR WHAT?

A MOUTHFUL OF FACTS

A COLLECTION OF BITE-SIZED FACTS AND STATS ABOUT TEETH AND MOUTHS. BITING STUFF!

THE AVERAGE PERSON has 32 teeth: 12 molars, 8 incisors, 8 premolars, and 4 canines.

FIFTY PER CENT of people say that the first thing they notice about someone is their smile – **SO BRUSH WELL!**

In the past, toothbrush bristles were made from the hair of cows and pigs.

Tooth enamel is the hardest thing in the human body.

AMERICANS buy 53 million litres (14 million gallons) of toothpaste every year.

A BEAVER'S TEETH never stop growing.

WEIGHING up to 5.4 kg (12 lb) each, the molars of an African elephant are as heavy as watermelons.

GIRAFFES each have 32 teeth, the same number as humans. But they only have front teeth on their bottom jaw. The rest are back teeth.

BIRDS don't have teeth, though they do have a bone in the tongue. Weird.

ALL SNAKES have teeth, but they aren't used for chewing. Snakes swallow their victims whole and have backwards-slanted teeth to make sure the victim doesn't slip back out.

MINNOWS (FRESHWATER FISH) have teeth in their throats.

THE DANDELION FLOWER got its name because its jagged leaf looks like a lion's tooth (*dent de lion* in French).

THE GAMES WE PLAYED

Games – you've got to love them. Kids have played games forever. Here are a few old games played way back when Grandpa was a lad.

EPHEDRISMOS

This game, played in ancient Greece, can get a bit physical. Two players put a medium-sized, but not too heavy, stone on the ground, then step back and throw other stones at it. The first player to knock over the main stone is the winner. This is where it gets fun – the winner gets to ride on the loser's back, covering the loser's eyes. The pair then run around until the losing player steps on the stone.

QUEEK

Queek was played by European children in the Middle Ages. A large, checkered cloth – like a giant, soft chessboard – is laid on the ground. Players then take turns calling out black or white, and then toss pebbles onto the board, trying to get their pebble to land on the colour square they called out.

STOOP BALL

Popularized in New York City after World War I, stoop ball is a street version of baseball played with a rubber ball known as a "pinkie". One player, the "batter", throws the ball at the edge of the stoop (a set of steps). The other players, the "fielders", try to catch the ball before it bounces. For every time the ball bounces before it's caught, the batter scores a point. If someone catches it, the batter is out and the person who caught it is next to bat.

HANETSUKI

This traditional Japanese game is a lot like badminton – but with no net. It's often played by girls before the new year. By tradition, the longer the girls are able to keep the shuttlecock (that's the little thing you hit back and forth) in the air, the less annoying the mosquitoes will be during the coming year.

HAWK CATCHING THE CHICKS

Kids in China have been playing this game for hundreds of years. When the game begins, one child is chosen to be the hawk and one is chosen to be the hen. All the other kids hold hands – they're the chicks. The hawk tries to catch the chicks and the hen tries to protect them.

MAGIC

LEVITATE!

This simple trick is called the Balducci levitation and it's sure to impress. Get a friend to stand about 3 m (10 ft) behind you. Turn one foot out at an angle so your friend can see the whole foot, but only the heel of the other. Raise the visible foot while going on tiptoe with the other foot. Do it slowly, as though it takes enormous effort to defy gravity. Then drop down suddenly before your friend figures it out. They'll be stunned!

IS THIS YOUR CARD?

This is a fiendishly clever but very easy card trick. You need an ordinary pack of cards. While shuffling the pack, take a sneaky look at the bottom card and commit it to memory. Fan out the cards and ask a friend to "pick a card, any card, and memorize it". Ask them to place the card on top of the pack, and tell them to cut the pack wherever they like. Now simply pick up the cards and look for the one you memorized. Whichever card is in front of it is your friend's card. Tah-dah!

TRICKS

COIN SWITCH

Ask a friend for a coin. Take it with your right hand and, so the audience can see, place it in the palm of your left hand. Here's the tricky part: in one quick motion, turn your hands into fists while quickly throwing the coin from your left hand to your right hand. If you do it quickly enough, the audience won't notice the toss. Now open your hands and show them that the coin has magically switched from one hand to another.

MAGIC PENCIL

Here's a simple one, and all you need is a pencil. Grab your wrist with one hand and use the other hand to pick up the pencil. Then, with your "grabbing" hand, secretly extend your index finger and pin the pencil to the palm of your hand. Slowly open that hand, showing only the back of it to the audience. To them, it'll look like the pencil is magically stuck to your palm!

THINGS THEY SAY IN
HOLLYWOOD

"A celebrity is a person who works hard all his life to become well known, then wears dark glasses to avoid being recognized."

Fred Allen (comedian)

"I know very little about acting. I'm just an incredibly gifted faker."

Robert Downey, Jr. (faker)

"Hollywood is a place where they'll pay you a thousand dollars for a kiss and fifty cents for your soul."

Marilyn Monroe (Hollywood icon)

"The length of a film should be directly related to the endurance of the human bladder."

Alfred Hitchcock (film director)

"My movies were the kind they show in prisons and on airplanes, because nobody can leave."

Burt Reynolds (actor) about his less-successful films

"I dream for a living."

Steven Spielberg (film director)

"I could take Sean Connery in a fight... I could definitely take him."

Harrison Ford (actor)

39

A BRIEF HISTORY OF TELEVISION

THE OLDEN DAYS

There were loads of inventions, discoveries, and experiments that resulted in the thing we now call television. But if you want to put an exact date on the beginning of TV, it's **1 September 1928**. That's when American inventor **Philo Farnsworth** demonstrated an early version of a working electronic television.

In 1939 Farnsworth sold all of his television patents to RCA Victor for **$1 million.** The sets debuted at the **New York World's Fair**, and electronic televisions were available to the public soon after. The age of TV had begun!

WHERE'S THE REMOTE?!

The first wireless remote – the **Philco Mystery Control (1939)** – was actually for use with radios. The first TV remote debuted in **1950** and connected to the TV set via a wire. Its name? **The Lazy Bones**. It was a cool gadget in its day, but consumers complained about tripping over the wires. So in **1955** the **Flashmatic** hit the stores – the first ever wireless TV remote.

COLOUR

Researchers at the US TV network CBS invented the colour TV set in **1940**. The picture quality was poor at first, and only a handful of the new sets were bought, though black-and-white TVs had sold tens of millions. Ultimately the CBS system failed, but in **1953** RCA swooped in with a better quality machine and colour TV was here to stay.

THE BEEB

The British Broadcasting Corporation (**BBC**) started broadcasting TV programmes in 1929, only four years or so after Scottish engineer **John Logie Baird** had invented the television. Broadcasts were suspended in 1939 because they would have provided a radio beacon to German bombers in World War II. They resumed in 1946.

HD

High-definition television (**HDTV**) hit the market in **1998**, offering sports fans, technology lovers, and movie buffs a revolution in picture quality and sound.

THEY SAID WHAT?

"**The problem with television is that the people must sit and keep their eyes glued on a screen; the average American family hasn't time for it… for this reason, if for no other, television will never be a serious competitor of broadcasting.**"

The New York Times, 1939

TV FIRSTS

The word "television'" was coined in 1902.
The first face ever to appear on TV was that of a ventriloquist's dummy in 1925.
The first frozen TV dinner hit the shops in 1945.
The first soap opera on TV – *War Bride* – was broadcast in the summer of 1946.
At midnight on 1 August 1981, the first music video premiered on MTV – *Video Killed the Radio Star* by The Buggles.
The Walt Disney cartoon *Donald's Cousin Gus* was the first cartoon to appear on TV. It debuted on 19 May 1939 in the US.

OUR POPULAR WORLD

A LOOK AT SOME OF THE THINGS PEOPLE LIKE BEST

☞ **MOST WATCHED SPORTING EVENT**

FOOTBALL WORLD CUP

☞ **MOST COMMON NAME**

MUHAMMAD

☞ **MOST POPULAR ICE CREAM FLAVOUR**

VANILLA

☞ **MOST COMMON LAST NAME**

CHANG

☞ **MOST POPULAR TOY**

Sorry Barbie, not you this time. **IT'S LEGO!** Since everyone's favourite interlocking blocks first hit the shops in 1949, over 20 billion have been made per year – that's **600 PER SECOND!**

☞ **BESTSELLING MUSIC ARTIST/GROUP**

THE BEATLES

☞ **MOST POPULAR SPICE**

Simple old **BLACK PEPPER**.

AMAZING!

MOST POPULAR BEVERAGE

After water, **IT'S TEA**. Close to **20 BILLION CUPS** of tea are drunk every day!

MOST POPULAR CAR COLOUR

SILVER

COOL!

MOST POPULAR EMAIL SERVICE

YAHOO. **256.2 MILLION PEOPLE** have accounts.

MOST POPULAR HOT DOG TOPPING

MUSTARD

MOST POPULAR SPORTS TEAM

MANCHESTER UNITED

MOST POPULAR CHOCOLATE BAR

SNICKERS

TOP FIZZY DRINK

COCA-COLA, by a landside. They sell more than **683 MILLION DRINKS PER DAY!**

MOST VISITED MUSEUM

THE LOUVRE in Paris. Over **5 MILLION PEOPLE** visit this famous museum, home to the *Mona Lisa*, **EVERY YEAR!**

WOW!

BODY LANGUAGE

So much can be given away by a LOOK or a GESTURE. Want to know what people are really saying? **Here's an insight into the body's secret code!**

ALL EYES ON YOU

Your feelings can be given away by an upturned or downturned mouth – but the eyes are just as important. As they say, **"Eyes are the window to the soul".**

- A furrowed brow: **mean and mischievous.**

- Eyebrows raised in the middle: **sad**

- **Eyes wide open: afraid**

CROSSED ARMS

One of the most basic and easily recognizable body-language signs is when someone crosses their arms across their chest. This usually means they're unconsciously **putting up a wall** around themselves – most likely because they're scared or uncomfortable. On the other hand, they could simply be cold...

THE MIRROR GAME

When we're being friendly, we tend to **imitate** other people's movements subconsciously. You can try this out for yourself! Start a conversation with a friend and try to **mirror** what they do. But don't be too obvious about it. Then, after a little while, do a test: run your hand through your hair or scratch your chin. If they do the same thing, then you've got them! You're seeing body language in action.

PEOPLE MIGHT BE LYING TO YOU IF:

- They avoid **eye contact** with you
- They keep touching their **face**, **mouth**, and **throat** with their hands
- They **blink** a lot
- The **timing** doesn't match between their words and gestures. For example, if someone opens a present and says "Perfect!", then a moment later they smile – that's a lie.

BODACIOUS BODY LANGUAGE

Some researchers think that non-verbal signals make up 80 per cent of all communication. One scientist has even claimed that only seven per cent of a conversation comes from spoken words. So sit up straight and make eye contact!

7'0

6'0

5'0

4'0

FOILED!
A British gang had big plans to break into a branch of the Royal Bank of Scotland. Sadly for them, they drilled into the empty office next door instead of the bank.

SORRY, WE'RE CLOSED
Amateur criminal Christopher Allen Koch planned to rob the Pennsylvania Citizens & Northern Bank, but didn't realize it closed at noon! Employees spotted him trying to open the locked door – then gave the cops his car number plate.

BAD FIRST DATE
Bumbling, broken-hearted Brent Brown robbed an 18-year-old pizza delivery girl – then called her later and asked her out on a date! Not surprisingly, she said no. But she did give his number to the cops. They said yes… to arresting him.

46

Some **CRIMINALS** are **MAD** masterminds – at least, that's how they're portrayed in the movies. In reality the common crook is **JUST PLAIN STUPID...**

KARATE

One unfortunate thief attempted to break into a Colombian house, not realizing it was the home of Pan-American karate master Cristian Garces and her instructors. They spotted the burglar and proceeded to karate chop him into submission until the police arrived.

POSITIVE ID

A man from Indiana, USA, gave police officers a fake name after being pulled over. He was caught out when they noticed his real name – Cecil – tattooed across his neck.

PIZZA THE ACTION

Alejandro Martinez filled out a job-application form at a Las Vegas pizza joint, then immediately decided to rob the place. It didn't take police long to find him – he had put his real name and address on the job application!

LEFT SOMETHING BEHIND?

Yet another man from Indiana, USA, robbed a grocery store. He grabbed the money and ran – but left his wallet on the counter!

47

GAMES

TO PLAY IN THE CAR

"Are we nearly there yet?"...

You'll be wishing the car journey were longer with these **cool car games.**

FIND FIFTY Everyone in the car (except the driver) pick something and try to find 50 of it. For example: blue cars, dogs, or cyclists. It's a race: the first to 50 wins.

TRAVEL TIP!
If you tend to get carsick, take frequent breaks from reading or playing video games and look out of the window.

I SPY First, pick something in the car that everyone can see. Then give a hint by saying what letter it begins with. Then everyone else gets to have a guess. Whoever guesses correctly first is the new spy and gets to pick.

THE NUMBER-PLATE GAME

Spot a car number plate and shout out its letters – then everyone in the car tries to come up with a **funny phrase** using those letters. If the plate reads TGR, you could say **"THIS GAME ROCKS"**!

48

SCAVENGER HUNT

Before you begin your trip, come up with a scavenger-hunt list. You can use one list and work together or give everybody their own list and make it a competition.

Here are a few sample things to get your hunt started:

- **Motorbike**
- **Service station**
- **Police car**
- **Roadworks**
- **Car pulling a boat**

First one to tick off each item on the list wins!

THE ULTIMATE CAR GAME

This is the ultimate game of the car-journey universe. You'll need a pen and paper. Make a list of things and assign them points. For example,

1. **A COW = 1 POINT**
2. **PLANE = 10 POINTS**
3. **CONVERTIBLE = 20 POINTS**
4. **BOAT = 25 POINTS**
5. **HORSE TRAILER = 50 POINTS**

Keep your eyes open for **CEMETERIES**, because that's where it gets interesting. The first person to spot a cemetery gets to wipe out all the points of one other player. So if you spot the cemetery, you can set your annoying brother back to zero! But be careful – whoever spots the next cemetery can wipe **YOU** out!

HISTORY'S GREATEST EVER SCAMS & HOAXES

You've got to be joking...? And yes they were. Here are some of the best scams and hoaxes ever. Can you believe anybody got away with them?

"IF YOU BELIEVE THAT, I HAVE A BRIDGE TO SELL YOU."

Ever heard that phrase? It means you're gullible, and it's inspired by US fraudster George Parker, one of the most notorious conmen in history. His scam was simple: sell famous property that he didn't own, like New York's Statue of Liberty and Brooklyn Bridge. He was convicted of fraud only three times – even though he reportedly "sold" the Brooklyn Bridge more than twice a week! But his luck eventually ran out, and after his third conviction in 1928 he went to prison for life. Perhaps it was a bridge too far.

NESSIE AND THE SURGEON'S PHOTO

The famous Loch Ness Monster is a mythical creature said to inhabit Scotland's Loch Ness. It's been the subject of many legends and hoaxes – none greater than the so-called surgeon's photo, first published in 1934. British surgeon Robert Kenneth Wilson claimed to have taken the photo of Nessie's head and neck rising out of the water. The photo was originally submitted anonymously, so it became known as simply the surgeon's photo. In 1994 the truth was revealed: the monster was just a toy submarine with a head and neck made of modelling clay.

THE MARTIANS ARE COMING!

On 30 October 1938 a US radio broadcast caused panic with a dramatic newsflash announcing that Martians were invading Earth in giant tripods and attacking people with heat rays. The live broadcast was actually a dramatization of the classic sci-fi novel *War of the Worlds* directed and narrated by Hollywood legend Orson Welles. It was so realistic that listeners who tuned in halfway through the show thought the fake news bulletins were true. Even though it was never intended to fool people, it has been called the single greatest media hoax of all time.

THE TURK... CHECKMATE!

A mechanical man that was also ace at chess? Not possible, right? Well, it had the world fooled for years. Built by Wolfgang von Kempelen, "the Turk" toured Europe and America in the late 18th century, defeating chess masters and statesmen (including Napoleon Bonaparte and Benjamin Franklin), and baffling everyone along the way. From the waist up, the chess-playing robot looked human, complete with Turkish robes, a turban, and even a pipe. Beneath that was a cabinet containing all sorts of gears and wheels that made clockwork noises. But this was all a front. Hiding inside was a man who pulled on levers to operate the Turk's arms and make him shake his head at opponents or say *Échec!* (French for "check"). The Turk's secret was kept for over 80 years until the robot was destroyed in a fire and its final owner revealed the truth.

ANIMAL FACT-O-PEDIA

Most elephants weigh less than the tongue of a blue whale.

Polar bears are left-handed.

FLAMINGOS ARE PINK BECAUSE THEY EAT A LOT OF SHRIMPS.

A group of kangaroos is called a mob.

Koalas sleep for 20 hours a day.

It's not just a tiger's fur that's striped – its skin is too!

Pigs can get sunburnt.

The Basenji is the only breed of dog that doesn't bark.

A woodpecker can peck 20 times per second. And despite all that pecking, it never gets headaches thanks to air pockets in its skull that cushion its (super-small) brain.

Camels have three eyelids.

A bear can run at speeds of up to 30 mph (50 km/h).

Cheetahs and pumas are the only big cats that don't roar – they make mewing noises like house cats.

An earthworm is like one big tongue – its body is covered in taste sensors.

Armadillos can walk underwater to cross streams and rivers.

Butterflies have taste sensors on the bottom of their feet. They taste their food by standing on it.

An ostrich's eye is bigger than its brain.

WHAT WAS built WHEN?

THEY MAY LOOK LIKE CRUMBLING RUINS TODAY –
but at the time these were engineering masterpieces!
Here's a quick look to see who was building what, when.

488 BCE
Parthenon
GREECE

3000 BCE
Stonehenge
ENGLAND

100 BCE
Petra
JORDAN

70 CE
Roman Colosseum
ITALY

← BCE

500 BCE
Persepolis
IRAN

537 CE
Hagia Sophia
Cathedral
ISTANBUL

3200 BCE
The Great
Pyramid
EGYPT

220 BCE
The Great Wall
of China
CHINA

600 CE
Chichen Itza
(Mayan civilization)
MEXICO

54

691 CE
Dome of the Rock
ISRAEL

1708 CE
St Paul's
Cathedral
ENGLAND

1845 CE
Suez Canal
EGYPT

1931 CE
Empire State
Building
USA

798 CE
Kiyomizu-dera
JAPAN

1806 CE
Arc de
Triomphe
PARIS

1889 CE
Eiffel
Tower
PARIS

1648 CE
Taj Mahal
INDIA

CE

1406 CE
The Forbidden City
CHINA

1800 CE
The White House
USA

1886 CE
Statue of
Liberty
USA

1450 CE
Machu Picchu
(Incan civilization)
PERU

1846 CE
Trafalgar Square
ENGLAND

55

QUICK PSYCHOLOGY

Here's a quick guide to understanding psychology and some fun ways to use it in everyday life.

Subliminal messages

These are messages hidden within something else, so only your unconscious is able to see them. Here's an example: in 1957, a drive-in cinema flashed the words **DRINK COCA-COLA** and **EAT POPCORN** for $\frac{1}{3000}$ of a second, every 5 seconds. They claim to have sold almost 60% more popcorn thanks to the subliminal ad.

Ivan Pavlov (1849–1936)

Pavlov was the first person to have the idea of classical conditioning, which means learning through association. For example, if you hear the **ICE CREAM** van, do you suddenly feel hungry? If you do, that's because you've been conditioned to associate the sound of the **ICE CREAM** van with eating ice cream.

Analyze your dreams

Dreams often feature things that are occupying your mind, so what are they telling you?

- **Being chased.** This common nightmare means you're feeling threatened by someone or by an emotion.
- **Being lost.** Something in your life is troubling you and you don't know what to do.

B.F. Skinner (1904–1990)

Skinner was best known for his work in the field of **BEHAVIOURISM** (studying people based on how they react to their **ENVIRONMENT**). Skinner thought that nearly all of our emotions were controlled by habit, and that they could be learned or unlearned.

Reverse psychology

This is a fun one to use in your everyday life. Reverse psychology is when you do something and hope to get the opposite reaction. For example, if you have a **REALLY HORRIBLE SANDWICH** for lunch and you want to get your friend to taste it, tell them they can't have any. Pretty soon, **they'll be begging you for a bite!**

Sigmund Freud (1856–1939)

Austrian psychiatrist Sigmund Freud introduced the idea of the unconscious – a part of your mind that you're not aware of. Ever heard someone refer to something as a **"Freudian slip?"** That's when someone makes a verbal slip-up that may actually reveal their inner feelings.

PLANETS OF THE
SOLAR SYSTEM

There are eight planets in our solar system. The inner solar system contains those planets closest to the Sun: **MERCURY, VENUS, EARTH,** and **MARS.** The outer solar system contains the gas giants: **JUPITER, SATURN, URANUS,** and **NEPTUNE.**

Mercury

Mercury is similar in appearance to our Moon. It's the closest to the Sun and the smallest of the eight planets. It takes Mercury 59 days to rotate on its axis, but only 88 days to orbit the Sun – which means there are 1.49 days in a Mercury year!

Venus

Venus is small and rocky, and is surrounded by thick yellow clouds. Unlike Earth clouds, which are made of water, Venus's clouds are made from poisonous sulphuric acid. The poisonous clouds reflect so much sunlight, Venus shines like a star.

Earth

It's the third rock from the Sun! As far as we know right now, Earth is the only planet that supports life. The Earth's core is one of the hottest things in the Universe. Earth is over 4.5 billion years old. Oh yeah, and it's where we live!

Mars

Mars, "the Red Planet", is home to Olympus Mons (Latin for "Mount Olympus"), the largest mountain in the known Universe. It's roughly 26,875 m (88,176 ft) high – three times as tall as Mount Everest! Mars was named after the Roman god of war.

WHAT ABOUT PLUTO?

For a long time **Pluto** was considered to be the ninth planet. But it's so small that scientists recently downgraded it to a **"dwarf planet"**, making it no longer one of the official planets in our solar system.

Jupiter

Jupiter is easily the largest of the planets. It's so big, you could fit 1,000 Earths inside it! Jupiter is one of the gas giants and is made up of hydrogen and helium. It is home to the "Great Red Spot", a violent storm of swirling gas that's hundreds of years old.

Saturn

Saturn is a gas giant, and is circled by thousands of bright, glowing rings. The rings are made of millions of particles ranging in size from a centimetre to a few metres. Saturn has more moons than any other planet – 18.

Uranus

The gas giant Uranus is made of rock and ice, and is coloured blue by the methane in its atmosphere. Uranus is unique because it is tilted sideways. When it was visited by *Voyager 2* in 1986, its south pole was pointed at the Sun.

Neptune

The gas planet Neptune has the fastest winds in the solar system, reaching speeds of up to 2,000 km/h (1,240 mph). Neptune was discovered in 1846 and it has still yet to make a complete orbit around the Sun. That's one long year!

SCALY!
THE WILD WORLD OF REPTILES

FIRST OF ALL: WHAT MAKES A REPTILE A REPTILE? HERE ARE THE TWO BIGGEST CLUES:

1. They're covered in scales.

2. They're cold-blooded (which doesn't mean their blood is necessarily cold, just that their body temperature changes with their surroundings).

QUESTION?

There are 8,240 reptile species in the world, creeping around every continent but one. Can you guess which continent?

Answers on p. 126

SNAKES

• There are **3,000 TYPES OF SNAKES** in the world, but only about 40 of those are dangerous to humans. In fact, more Americans die from bee stings each year than from snakebites.

• But be careful if you're in Australia – it's the only place in the world where there are more **POISONOUS** snakes than non-poisonous snakes.

THE KING COBRA is the biggest of the baddies – this poisonous snake can grow to 5.5 m (18 ft) long and can weigh more than 9 kg (20 lb).

• Look, no nose! Snakes and lizards smell by flicking their tongues into the air and capturing scent molecules.

SCALY!
Reptile scales are made of the same stuff as your hair.

LIZARDS

TALL AND SMALL

The world's largest lizard is Indonesia's Komodo dragon, which can reach 3 m (10 ft) in length. The smallest lizard is the dwarf gecko of the Virgin Islands. At a mere 16 mm (¾ in) long from snout to tail, this miniature reptile is small enough to fit on a coin.

TRIVIA FACTS

THINK YOUR PARENTS ARE OLD?

Some turtles live to be more than 150 years old!

CROCODILES

- **WATCH OUT!** In the water, Nile crocodiles can reach speeds of up to 47 km/h (29 mph).

- Crocodiles can't stick out their tongues. **SO THERE!**

- Crocodiles are able to grow new teeth to replace their old teeth. **NO TRIPS** to the **DENTIST**, which is probably good – what dentist would want to stick a hand in a **CROC'S MOUTH?**

DON'T FEAR THE PHOBIA

PHOBOPHOBIA is the fear of phobias!

PHILEMAPHOBIA is the fear of kissing. And not just having to kiss your aunt Selma – kissing anyone!

PARASKAVEDEKATRIAPHOBIA is the fear of Friday the 13th (the day and the movie).

CAN YOU GUESS WHAT THESE PHOBIAS ARE?

- **TELEPHONOPHOBIA**
- **AMNESIPHOBIA**
- **NUDOPHOBIA**
- **SOMNIPHOBIA**
- **CARNOPHOBIA**
- **BIBLIOPHOBIA**

Answers on p. 126

SCAREDY-CAT? DOES THE IDEA OF AN 8-LEGGED CREEPY-CRAWLY FREAK YOU OUT? DON'T WORRY, THERE ARE EVEN DAFTER THINGS TO BE AFRAID OF. TAKE A LOOK AT THESE!

CONSECOTALEOPHOBIA is the fear of chopsticks.

COULROPHOBIA is one of the most common phobias: the fear of clowns. Johnny Depp and Daniel "Harry Potter" Radcliffe are both coulrophobics.

ARACHIBUTYROPHOBIA is the fear of peanut butter sticking to the roof of the mouth.

ALEKTOROPHOBIA is the fear of chickens.

HIPPOPOTOMONSTROSESQUIPEDALIOPHOBIA is the fear of long words. For real. No, seriously.

ALLIUMPHOBIA is the fear of garlic. Vampires are alliumphobic, and if vampires scare you, you are sanguivoriphobic!

63

SUPER-SLOPPY-SCIENCE
EXPERIMENTS

READY TO GET MESSY? Here are some super-fun, super-sloppy science experiments you can try at home. Make sure you have adult supervision!

COLA BOTTLE VOLCANO

WHAT YOU NEED:
- Large bottle of diet cola
- Packet of mint imperials

DO IT:
1 **STEP ONE: GO OUTSIDE!** If you do this experiment inside, your mum will hit the roof.
2 Stand the cola bottle on flat ground for a few minutes so the fizzy liquid can settle. Then carefully remove the lid.
3 Now comes the tricky bit. You need to drop all the mints into the bottle at once. To make this easier, you could tape the mints together to make a long stack or you could drop them through a cardboard tube or funnel.
4 As soon as you've dropped in the mints, get out of the way!

THE SCIENCE BEHIND THE MESS
Fizzy drinks get their bubbles from the gas carbon dioxide, which is dissolved in the liquid and forms bubbles as it escapes. The rough surface of the mint imperials encourages bubbles to form more quickly than usual. When you put a whole packet in, so many bubbles form that the drink turns to foam and explodes.

YUCKY PUTTY

WHAT YOU NEED:
- 50g (¼ cup) cornflour
- 60ml (¼ cup) water
- mixing bowl

DO IT:
1. Put the cornflour in the bowl. Add food colouring if you want.
2. Slowly stir in the water, mixing thoroughly.
3. Let the mixture stand for a couple minutes.

Now it's time to have fun. Scoop up a handful and squeeze it in your palm – it will turn solid. Now let your hand relax – the yucky putty turns back into a liquid!

THE SCIENCE BEHIND THE MESS
Yucky putty is a non-Newtonian fluid, which means that its viscosity (how runny it is) depends on how much force is being applied to it. When you apply a sudden force, it turns hard. When there's no force, it turns liquid again. Quicksand is another non-Newtonian fluid, but it works the opposite way. If you get stuck and try to escape, it turns harder, holding you firm and trapping you!

BEST

The BEST things ever said about COMPUTERS

Joel Makower [1984]

Business analyst

"For every computer error, there are at least two human errors, one of which is blaming it on the computer."

Ken Olsen [1977]

President of Digital Equipment Corporation

"There is no reason for any individual to have a computer in their home."

Pablo Picasso [1881–1973]

Painter

"Computers are useless. They can only give you answers."

Grace Murray Hopper [1945]

On the removal of a two-inch long moth from an experimental computer at Harvard:

"From then on, when anything went wrong with a computer, we said it had bugs in it."

66

Winn Schwartau [1994]

Computer expert

"Software is what makes your computer behave and look smarter than it is."

Mr. Azae [1957]

Television executive, to computer designer Richard Sumner in the great Spencer Tracy/ Katharine Hepburn movie *Desk Set*.

"I don't understand a word you're saying, but it sounds great."

David D. Thornburg [1985]

Writer

"Who has such a large Christmas card mailing list that you need to keep it on a computer? If so, why aren't I on it?"

Gene DeWeese [1984]

Sci-Fi author

"The first digital computer, of course, was a set of ten fingers that somebody realized could be used for counting."

Thomas J. Watson [1943]

Chairman of IBM

"I think there is a world market for about five computers."

Bruce Knapp [1984]

Commenting on the role of supercomputers:

"It means you can try to answer questions you thought the universe was going to do without."

101 cures for BOREDOM

Bored? Bored of being bored? Here are 101 ways to escape the boring prison of King Bore and his Boredomian Army.

1. Search for belly button fluff.
2. Draw your family tree – see how many generations back you can go.
3. Learn to whistle.
4. Make hand-shadow puppets.
5. Write a short story.
6. Read a short story.
7. Write a rap about your short story.
8. Try doing everything with your "other" hand.
9. Prepare and serve a three-course dinner.
10. Plant some seeds.
11. Teach yourself to burp on command.
12. Write your memoirs in rhyme.
13. Count the number of hairs in one square centimetre of your arm.
14. Write a note to the head of your country.
15. Make a list of 20 things that make you angry.
16. Now make a list of 20 things that make you happy.
17. Make a list of 20 things you are proud of.
18. Make a list of 20 things you are ashamed of.
19. Count 1,000 somethings – like trees, pebbles, coins, ideas, people, or leaves.
20. Make a list of the top ten things you want to do in your life.
21. Write an original joke.
22. Learn your favourite poem.
23. Come up with your own 101 somethings, write them down, and send them to this book's publisher for possible inclusion in our next edition.
24. Think of a cool new nickname for yourself.
25. Play a game of patience.
26. Skim a pebble.
27. Juggle. (Can't? Turn to p. 72)
28. Toss a ball in the air and catch it. How many times can you catch it without dropping?
29. Write a song.
30. Plan your dream house.
31. Memorize a famous speech.
32. Invent a sandwich.
33. Make a house of cards.
34. Clean up your room.
35. Learn to tie a new knot.
36. Make a movie.
37. Build a fort.
38. Start keeping a journal.
39. Twiddle your thumbs.
40. Watch a funny video on YouTube.
41. Measure how far you can spit.
42. Say the alphabet backwards.
43. Draw yourself in the mirror.
44. Take photos.
45. Learn how to cook a fun and easy meal.
46. Rearrange your bedroom.
47. Learn about the history of where you live.
48. Make breakfast in bed for your parents.
49. Learn to stand on your head, cartwheel, and forward roll.
50. Create a costume out of your clothes.

51. Draw the view from your bedroom window.

52. Take a bath.

53. Talk to yourself.

54. Make up a secret handshake.

55. Try out a new hairstyle.

56. Exercise.

57. Make a collage.

58. Decorate a T-shirt.

59. Tell all your friends about this amazing new book you're reading (y'know, this book in your hands!)

60. Learn the definition of a new word and use it in a sentence.

61. Draw a floor plan for an awesome tree house.

62. Cut out black-and-white pictures from magazines and colour them in.

63. Write a poem.

64. Flip a coin 10 times, 50 times, 100 times – what comes up more often?

65. Rename the constellations (they are VERY out of date).

66. Invent a superhero with a completely original power.

67. Learn the alphabet in French or Spanish or Greek or all three.

68. Invent a word.

69. Invent a word that perfectly describes your mood or feelings right now.

70. Invent a word that perfectly describes you.

71. Invent a word that sounds like what the word means, like BANG or POP.

72. Design a business card for yourself.

73. Imagine yourself at 70 years old. Now write a biography of yourself.

74. Figure out the five best places to hide money should anybody ever break into your home.

75. Go and look in those five places to see if anybody ever hid money there and forgot about it.

76. Invent a secret code for writing covert messages to your friends.

77. Invent a secret language and start using it with friends.

78. Invent a club, decide who'd be in it, and write its rules.

79. Write a letter to yourself, then put it away to open in ten years.

80. Make a paper aeroplane. Make two and race them.

81. Turn all the lights off and pretend you're camping in a wild jungle.

82. Find a rock in your garden and see if there's an earwig hiding under it.

83. Make ice cubes out of fruit juice or a fizzy drink.

84. Make a sock-puppet hero and a sock-puppet monster. Then make them battle.

85. Make a telephone out of two cups and some string.

86. Create a stand-up comedy routine. Perform it for your parents.

87. Blow up a balloon and play volleyball with a friend.

88. Make up an imaginary friend.

89. Come up with the ultimate chocolate bar. What would be in it? What would you call it?

90. Climb a tree.

91. Design and make a new game.

92. Create a new dance.

93. Get a BIG piece of paper and try to trace your entire body.

94. Measure the amount of steps from one place to another. For example, how many steps does it take to get from your bedroom to outside and back again?

95. Play connect the dots with the moles and freckles on your arm. Don't use permanent markers.

96. Choreograph a movie-style sword fight.

97. Play any sport – but use a Frisbee instead!

98. Find a mirror. Make the weirdest face possible. Go show someone.

99. Watch TV on mute and make up new words for the characters.

100. Try a new food.

101. Call someone just to talk.

OPTICAL ILLUSIONS

These visual enigmas play tricks with your mind, by confusing the way you see shapes and movement.

PENROSE TRIANGLE

At first glance this shape may look real, but look again – those angles are completely impossible!

MOVING IMAGE ILLUSIONS

These two pictures aren't really moving – are they? The patterns confuse your brain into **thinking** it sees movement just out of your focus, no matter where you look.

FALSE SPIRAL ILLUSION

Try tracing your finger around a curve of this "spiralling" shape, and you'll find that it's not a spiral at all, but a series of rings.

3-D ILLUSIONS

Both of these images use flat shapes to create an illusion of depth. 3-D boxes pop out at you from the picture on the right – but are the yellow shapes the tops of the cubes, or the bottoms?

HOW TO

WORLD RECORD THREE-BALL JUGGLE: 11 hours 4 minutes 22 seconds!

The best place to start if you want to be a clown is to learn to juggle. EASY! Well, let's see.

WHERE TO LEARN

The best place to learn is outside. Why? There's more space out there, and you're going to need it.

GETTING STARTED

First things first – you're going to need three juggling balls. Or three socks rolled into balls.

So you've got your three balls – now drop two. Get used to it. You'll be dropping a lot as you learn. Now with your one ball you're ready to start.

1. ONE-BALL ARCS

This is the most important skill to master and is the foundation of the whole juggling technique. Make sure you're standing comfortably, and throw the ball from your right hand to your left hand in a smooth arc. The ball should peak at eye level. Now throw it back from left hand to right. Keep this up until you can confidently and consistently arc the ball from right to left and back again.

JUGGLE

2. TWO-BALL SWITCH

You have now perfected the one-ball arc. Now, pick up a second ball. This part of the learning process is about timing. Stand comfortably with one ball in each hand. Make sure there is plenty of space around you. Throw the right-hand ball, as it reaches the top of the arc, throw the left-hand ball inside the arc of the first ball. Continue until you can throw and catch both balls.

3. THREE-BALL CYCLE

You can now throw and catch two balls. The next step is – you guessed it – the third ball. This step is all about rhythm. Hold two balls in your right hand, and one in your left. Perform the two-ball switch, and as the second ball reaches eye-level, throw the third ball (remember: inside the arc). You will definitely start to move about as you try to master this, so remember to practice outside.

4. FOREVER JUGGLING

With the three-ball cycle sorted you are nearly there. All that is left to do is to keep going. As you toss the third ball and it reaches the peak of its arc, throw ball number one, and start the cycle again. With a lot of practice, patience, and concentration you could juggle forever...

SUPER -LAME SUPER- HEROES

Everyone knows about Superman, Spiderman, and the Joker. But what about those less popular comic-book characters who gathered dust in attics and garages? Here we present some of the less fortunate, more obscure, and least successful superheroes.

MATTER-EATER LAD

Matter-Eater Lad is a member of the Legion of Super-Heroes. He has the ability to eat anything – absolutely anything! The Legion of Super-Heroes has actually employed a number of pretty lame superheroes over the years, including Bouncing Boy (he can bounce), Chlorophyll Kid (has the ability to make plants grow extra fast), and Infectious Lass (see facing page).

ZAN FROM THE WONDER TWINS

Zan had one of the most useless powers ever – the ability to turn into ice, water, or steam. And worst of all, his twin sister Zayna had an awesome power – she could turn into any animal, even a mythological one. So while Zan's stuck transforming into an ice cube, his sister can fly around as a griffin. Not fair.

MADAM FATAL

Despite the name, Madam Fatal was actually a man. Retired actor Richard Stanton dressed up as a little old lady and fought crime using his natural athleticism and supreme fighting skills. He used the little old lady get-up to catch villains off guard.

KITE MAN

This obscure Batman villain didn't really have any superpowers – he was just really, really good at hang-gliding. He was also armed with a whole bunch of kite-related weapons. Sadly, Kite Man is no longer with us – he was killed by Bruno Mannheim, a much cooler supervillain.

BROTHER POWER THE GEEK

This 60s superhero was a shop dummy that was struck by lightning, bringing him to life and giving him pretty much unlimited magic powers. He used his superpowers to… become a politician and run for the American government! Everyone realized how lame he was right away – he lasted all of two issues.

INFECTIOUS LASS

This DC Comics super heroine has the ability to give anyone a sickness or disease (only temporarily though). Say the Joker's about to rob a bank – she could give him the flu. Gotcha... Atchoo!

WHY IS THE
SKY BLUE?

Some things in life we take for granted. Grass is green and the sky is blue – but why? Here are a few answers to questions you may have wondered about.

Why does the wind blow?

When the Sun heats Earth, it also heats Earth's atmosphere. As the air gets warmer, it rises, and cold air moves in and replaces the hot air. That air movement is wind blowing!

Why do we have eyebrows?

Two reasons. Eyebrows keep sweat from running off your forehead and into your eyes, which can make it really hard to see. Also, they allow people to make facial expressions that other people can understand.

Why are mosquito bites soooo itchy?

Mosquitoes bite you so they can suck up your blood. But in order to keep your blood from clotting and drying up, they inject you with a little saliva when they bite. It's the chemicals in that saliva that make you so itchy.

Why is the sky blue?

Sunlight is made up of all the colours of the rainbow. As it travels through Earth's atmosphere towards us, it runs into trillions of tiny air molecules. Most of the different colours pass straight through the air, but blue light bounces off in a new direction when it strikes an air molecule. As a result, this light gets scattered right across the sky, making it look blue!

How are spiders able to walk up walls?

Two different ways. Some spiders have microscopic hairs on their feet that grasp the bumps and grooves in walls and ceilings. Other spiders daub their feet with the sticky silk that they use to make webs so they can cling to surfaces.

Why do leaves fall off trees in autumn?

Leaves harness the Sun's energy to make food so that trees can grow. But to do this they need lots of water. In winter, when the ground freezes, trees can't get enough water for the leaves, and there isn't much sunlight anyway. So trees with large, tender leaves let them die and fall off and then grow new ones in spring.

LIFE ON

EVERYBODY'S WONDERED ABOUT WHAT LIFE WOULD BE LIKE ON ANOTHER PLANET. But could humans actually go out and colonize another planet? Right now, no one knows for sure, but it's definitely a possibility.

Similarities to Earth

Recent unmanned missions to Mars have revealed the presence of water ice on Mars. So it appears the Red Planet has all the necessary elements to support life.

Unlike some planets in our solar system, Mars has an atmosphere. It's super-thin (roughly 1% of Earth's atmosphere) but it's strong enough to provide protection from the Sun's radiation.

The Martian day (known as a sol) is very close to Earth's – 24 hours and 39 minutes.

Mars has seasons like Earth, but they are twice as long because the Martian year is 669 sols.

NOW, WITH THAT SAID – THERE ARE STILL A LOT OF DIFFERENCES BETWEEN EARTH AND MARS THAT WILL MAKE COLONIZATION DIFFICULT.

MARS

THE MOST LIKELY CANDIDATE FOR
COLONIZATION BY HUMANS IS MARS.
It has water on it, and its atmosphere
is relatively similar to Earth's.
In 2007 NASA declared, "We hope to
discover if Mars can provide a
second home for humans..."

Differences to Earth

The surface gravity on Mars is about one-third that on Earth. It's amazing because you can kick a ball really, really far – but there are also health problems that go along with that level of weightlessness.

The Martian atmosphere contains the right gases, but in different amounts. Earth's atmosphere contains 78% nitrogen, 21% oxygen, and 0.038% carbon dioxide. Mars is mainly carbon dioxide (95%), with 2.7% nitrogen and only 0.13% oxygen.

Mars is way too cold – think Antarctica. Brrr!

Three-quarters of Earth's surface is water, but there are no large bodies of liquid water on Mars' surface.

TO MAKE MARS HABITABLE, WE NEED TO DO TWO MAJOR THINGS: ALTER THE ATMOSPHERE AND ADD HEAT.

So here's one crazy way to make MARS livable for humans – change it! Terraforming, which literally means "Earth-shaping", is the hypothetical process of changing a planet's temperature, atmosphere, ecology, and surface, to make it habitable for us human folk.

10 THINGS TO DO WITH A...
SPARE TYRE

Car tyres can take thousands of years to decompose, so rather than throw them away – recycle! Here are 10 things to do with a spare tyre.

MAKE A SANDPIT

FIND LOADS AND MAKE A HOUSE

MAKE A TYRE SWING

THROW A BALL THROUGH IT

GET TWO TYRES AND RACE THEM

STACK A FEW AND BUILD A FORT

FILL WITH WATER AND MAKE A MINI POND

USE IT AS A CHAIR FOR YOUR TREE HOUSE

SPLASH SOME PAINT ON IT – MODERN ART!

SHRED IT UP AND USE IT AS BOUNCY ARTIFICIAL TURF

TRASH OR TREASURE ?

10 THINGS TO DO WITH AN OLD SOCK

1. Make a sock puppet.
2. Make an entire sock puppet family and put on a show!
3. Cut off the end, decorate it, and make a cool wrist or arm band.
4. Secret safe! Hide stuff in it and stick it in your drawer – no one will ever think to look in there.
5. Stick a tennis ball inside it, tie it up, and make a great pet toy.
6. Put your hand in it and use it to dust your bedroom, your computer monitor, your TV – anything!
7. Cut four holes in it – hamster outfit.
8. Stuff it with beans, sew it up, and you've got a beanbag.
9. Sunglasses case.
10. Find three, roll them up – juggling balls!

10 THINGS TO DO WITH AN EMPTY PLASTIC BOTTLE

1. Get 10 of them and go bowling...
2. ... or play hoopla.
3. Draw a little door on it, fill it with action figures, and you've got a bathtub submarine!
4. Decorate it and make a pencil holder.
5. Fill it with pebbles and make a musical instrument.
6. Cut it in half, turn the bottom into a flowerpot, and give it to your mum as a gift.
7. Fill it with something heavy and make a door stop.
8. Ready-made piggy bank.
9. Gather all those sock puppets you made and play spin the bottle.
10. Perfect for filling water balloons in the middle of a water fight!

81

BEST THINGS EVER SAID BY
CARTOON
CHARACTERS

Cartoon characters look funny, have funny voices, and say the funniest things…

Porky Pig: **"TELL ME MR. HOLMES, WHERE DID YOU GO TO SCHOOL TO LEARN TO BE A DETECTIVE?"**

"I'LL RISE, BUT I WON'T SHINE."

Garfield the cat

Daffy Duck: **"ELEMENTARY, MY DEAR WATKINS. ELEMENTARY."**

Looney Tunes

"I DON'T KNOW! I DON'T KNOW WHY I DID IT, I DON'T KNOW WHY I ENJOYED IT, AND I DON'T KNOW WHY I'LL DO IT AGAIN!"

Bart Simpson, *The Simpsons*

"IF IT WASN'T FOR BAD LUCK, I'D HAVE NO LUCK AT ALL."

George Jetson, *The Jetsons*

"YABBA DABBA DOO!"

Fred Flintstone, *The Flintstones*

That's a job?

When I grow up I want to be a smell checker...

Yes, there is such a job! Don't feel like you have to restrict yourself to being a doctor, lawyer, or astronaut! Check out these crazy vocations.

Knife-thrower's assistant

Okay, this one definitely wins the award for scariest. But it's real. Professional knife throwers need someone to act as human targets in their stage acts. And if you've got the guts, that someone could be you!

HE STINKS!

PLEASE DON'T MIS THIS TIME!!

Smell checker

Like having your head in armpits all day? Then this could be the job for you. It's the responsibility of some laboratory researchers to do smell checks to make sure that antiperspirants and deodorants are actually doing their job. Hmmm...

Weed farmer

Some people actually grow weeds for a living. They then sell the plants to horticultural institutions and chemical research laboratories so they can can carry out tests to find the best way to kill them. Sounds barmy, but someone's got to do it.

Roller-coaster engineer

Now here's a fantastic job. Teams of roller coaster engineers design every part of a roller coaster – the loops, the drops, and the track – but you'll need to get a degree in engineering. School may not be fun, but it's worth it to get to ride the roller coasters first!

Master sniffer

George Aldrich is NASA's official "master sniffer". He has a staff of 25 people who smell everything that goes on a space shuttle. Things react differently in space, and no astronaut wants to be stuck with an awful smell – you can't open a window to get fresh air.

Dog-food tester

Simon Allison is a senior food technologist – who eats pet food for a living. Just like any other food, pet food needs to be tested. So, how does it taste? It's quite bland, really," Simon says. "Dogs enjoy all foods, while cats are more choosy."

Circus-elephant tender

Like elephants? Like the circus? Like HUGE piles of dung? If so, we've found your dream job. Elephant tenders take care of the animals behind the scenes – and that involves shovelling a lot of elephant poo. Not only is it disgusting – one elephant foot on your head, and you're a pancake.

HOW MUCH POO?

PIRATE-O-PEDIA

What exactly makes a pirate a pirate? Just dressing up in a daft outfit, not showering, and carrying a sword isn't enough. Real-life pirates were rough and tough types who travelled the high seas and plundered ships for gold, weapons, and other valuables. So, are you a sea dog or landlubber?

FAMOUS FICTIONAL PIRATE
Long John Silver – The villain of Robert Louis Stephenson's novel *Treasure Island*, Long John is the inspiration for much of today's pirate lore – he had a parrot, a peg leg, and walked using a crutch.

Dead Man's Chest isn't actually a chest – it's an island in the Caribbean Sea. Legend has it that Blackbeard stranded 15 of his crew there as punishment for mutiny.

FAMOUS FICTIONAL PIRATE
Captain Hook – Peter Pan's nemesis Captain Hook lost his hand to a hungry crocodile. While some real pirates had hooks, Captain Hook is responsible for the popular image of the hook-handed pirate.

BURIED TREASURE Did pirates always bury their treasure? In reality the only pirate known to have done this was William Kidd. He was a privateer for England (which meant he was officially licensed by the English government to attack enemy ships). Kidd buried his treasure in Long Island, New York before he was eventually captured and hanged.

Anne Bonny – Female pirates were rare and Anne Bonny was the most infamous of all of them! She was eventually captured and sentenced to execution, but then she completely disappeared. Some say she spent the rest of her life as a housewife.

The Jolly Roger
The Jolly Roger was the official pirate flag. It was a black flag with a white skull and crossbones. Scary? Well it was supposed to be...

Piece of eight
This is a Spanish one-ounce silver coin. It was roughly equivalent to 60 pence.

Why are pirates so mean? Because they Arrrrrr!

FAMOUS REAL PIRATE
Blackbeard – The vicious captain of the *Queen Anne's Revenge*, Blackbeard is probably the most famous of the real-life pirates. According to legend, he once shot his first mate because "if he didn't shoot one or two crewmen now and then, they'd forget who he was." Oh, and he had a black beard.

SUPERBUGS

People who study bugs are called **ENTOMOLOGISTS.**

Termites have **BACTERIA** in their stomachs to help them digest wood. Because these little stomach creatures produce a lot of methane, termites **FART** like crazy.

A **QUEEN ANT** can lay **30,000** eggs a month for up to 10 years.

ANTS CAN LIVE FOR 16 YEARS.

If you put **40 FIREFLIES** in a jam jar, you should be able to read by the **LIGHT THEY GIVE OFF.**

Fleas jump **130 TIMES** their own height. That's like a **PERSON JUMPING** over a 65-storey building.

If ants were **HUMAN SIZED**, they could run five times as fast as a record-breaking **OLYMPIC RUNNER.**

BUTTERFLIES HAVE 12,000 EYES.

The tiny silver eggs that mother lice stick to the hairs on a **LICE-INFECTED** head are called "nits". Nits often have to be removed by picking through each strand of hair. Thus the term **"NITPICKY"** for people who are very fussy.

Say this 10 times, fast: "Moths munch mushy mushrooms."

Some tarantulas can go for two years without eating.

Some people consider chocolate ants a delicacy.

Mosquitoes flap their wings 1,000 times a second.

The world's **SMALLEST SPIDER** is half the size of this **FULL STOP.**

ONLY FEMALE MOSQUITOES BITE YOU.

HORNETS EAT HOUSEFLIES.
Some American settlers used to hang hornets' nests in their homes to get rid of flies.

BEES are more likely to sting people on **WINDY DAYS** than in any other kind of weather.

Ghost stories

What's your favourite scary story? Here are some to share around a roaring fire, at the dead of night, on Halloween…

MIDNIGHT RIDE

It was a cloudy, moonless night. A young man named Ryan was driving home, when he passed a pretty young girl waiting by the side of the road. Being a nice guy, he pulled over and asked the girl if she needed a lift home. It was starting to rain and a chill was creeping through the air, so Ryan gave the girl his jacket to keep warm. Ryan asked the girl for her name. She was silent for a moment, then said it was Christina. They drove through the rain for an hour before they got to her house. Christina thanked Ryan for the ride, and he drove back home.

The next morning he realized that he had left his jacket with Christina. He drove back to Christina's house, but when he knocked on the door, an old woman answered. Ryan asked for Christina. The old woman said nothing, then angrily tried to slam the door in his face. That's when Ryan noticed a photo of Christina sitting on the mantel. "That's her!" Ryan said, pointing at the photo. The old woman's face turned white. "What is it?" Ryan asked.

The old woman told Ryan that her daughter had been dead for 15 years. In fact, she died 15 years ago, last night. Ryan couldn't believe it. "No, I need to see her grave", he said. Ryan got in his car and raced to the cemetery. Just steps inside, he saw a grave with the name Christina on it. And there, sitting on top of the gravestone, was his jacket.

My dearest Christina
R.I.P.

THE RMS *QUEEN MARY*

Could the RMS *Queen Mary I* really be haunted? Many people think so and some even claim to have seen the ghosts themselves!

The RMS *Queen Mary I* is a retired ocean liner that sailed the North Atlantic Ocean from 1936 to 1967. During World War II she carried thousands of troops across the Atlantic. During the war, she was painted grey to camouflage her on the high seas and she was known as the "Grey Ghost".

During her 60-year sailing history, 59 people died on board, and some of them still haunt the ship today. The pool area is the most haunted part of the ship. According to legend, a young girl tried to slide down the banister of the pool stairs, but a wave tossed the boat and she broke her neck when she fell. Her ghost now wanders the pool area, looking for her mother.

Crewman John Pedder was crushed by a huge steel door during an evacuation drill. Banging can often be heard coming from behind the door, and his ghost, clad in the blood-soaked blue overalls in which he died, is often seen wandering the corridor to the engine room. That's not all. Many people have reported hearing the sounds of little children crying coming from what was once the playroom.

So, could the ship really be haunted? The only way to know for sure is to go and visit the ship yourself. She's docked in California and you can take a tour.

Or are you too scared?

GO FISH! (2 TO 6 PLAYERS)

1 Deal each player seven cards (unless you have more than four players, then deal each player five cards).

2 Throw the rest of the cards into the middle of the table. This is the "fish pond" – the pool of cards you will be taking from throughout the rest of the game.

3 Choose a player to go first. Go by youngest, oldest, smelliest – it's up to you.

4 The goal of Go Fish is to collect the most sets of four, for example four kings, four tens, or four fours.

5 Whoever goes first (let's say it's you), ask another player for any card that you want, for example, a Jack. If the player you ask has that card, he or she must give it to you. Then you get to go again.

6 If not, he or she says **"Go Fish!"** and you then take a card from the pond. If you get the card you wanted, show everyone, and go again. If not, keep your card, and the player to your left gets a go.

7 Whenever you get a group of four, place it on the table in front of you. When the fish pond is empty, count up your foursomes. Whoever has the most wins.

CARDS

CRAZY CARD FACT!
Way back when, coins, cups, swords, and even sticks were used as suits.

SLAP JACK! (2 TO 8 PLAYERS)

1) Deal out all the cards. Each player should put their cards in a stack face down, so they can draw from them without looking at them.

2) The player to the left of the dealer goes first by taking the top card from his or her pile and tossing it face up in the middle of the table. When tossing a card, make sure you turn the card away from yourself so you don't see it before the other players. Do it quickly so no one has an advantage.

3) Play continues to the left until a Jack is thrown, then it's time to **Slap Jack!** Every player tries to slap the Jack. Whoever ever gets his or her hand down first wins and takes all the cards in the pile.

4) Continue playing. Each time a Jack is slapped the winner takes the pile. When players run out of cards from their original pile, they can use the cards won from the Slap Jack pile.

5) If you run out of cards and don't have a pile, then you're out. The game keeps going until one person has the entire deck.

6) Want to make the game a little more slappy? Don't just slap the Jacks, slap any picture card – Kings, Queens, even Aces.

THE INTERNET

A BRIEF HISTORY OF THE INTERNET

THE INTERNET STARTED IN THE LATE 1960s and early 1970s when the United States Defense Department begin researching ways to allow networks of computers to communicate with each other. The idea was to link government and university research centres and share information. As time passed, the network grew and grew until it included businesses, schools, companies, and ordinary people like you and me. Today over one-and-a-half billion people across the world are connected and interacting every day...

ALL VIA THE INTERNET!

INTERNET VIRUSES are programs or pieces of code that sneak onto your computer and then mess it up. Some are just annoying, causing programs to crash, but others can completely destroy a computer.

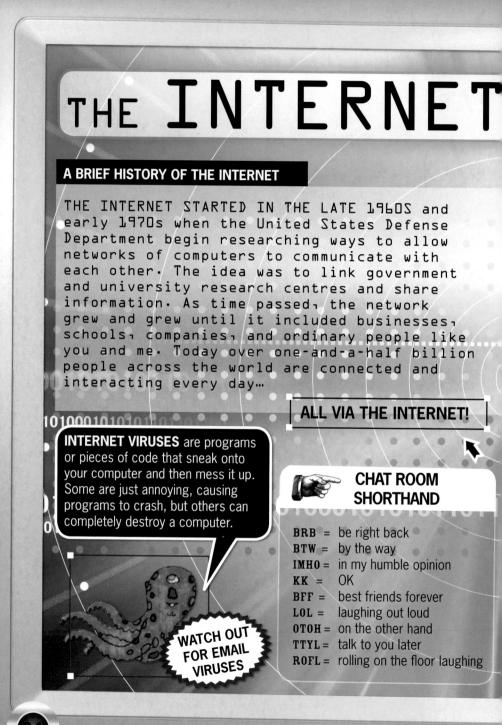

WATCH OUT FOR EMAIL VIRUSES

CHAT ROOM SHORTHAND

BRB	=	be right back
BTW	=	by the way
IMHO	=	in my humble opinion
KK	=	OK
BFF	=	best friends forever
LOL	=	laughing out loud
OTOH	=	on the other hand
TTYL	=	talk to you later
ROFL	=	rolling on the floor laughing

EVERYTHING YOU EVER WANTED TO KNOW ABOUT THE INTERNET AND THE WORLD WIDE WEB.

THE INTERNET VS. THE WORLD WIDE WEB

Despite what you might think, the Internet and the World Wide Web aren't the same thing. The **World Wide Web** is the system we use to access the Internet through browsers like Firefox and Internet Explorer. Think of it like this – the **Internet** is a **country** and the **World Wide Web** is the **capital**. Though if it were up to us, we'd name it **Webtown... or Webhampton!**

INTERNET FACTS

- **1 billion** users around the globe surf the Internet every month.
- There are more than **8 billion** internet pages, and counting!
- **80% of online shoppers are WOMEN.**
- One of the most amazing things about the Internet is that it's **not owned by any country, company, or corporation.**
- The Internet is growing super fast! It took only **5 years** for the Internet to reach **5 million users**. It took **38 years for radio to reach 5 million users and 13 years for TV!**
- Internet search company **Google** gets its name from the word **googol**, which represents the number 10,000,000,000,000,000, 000,000,000,000,000,000,000,000,000,000,000,000,000,000, 000,000,000,000,000,000,000,000,000,000,000,000,000,000.
- **86%** of people in **Iceland** are online.

FAMOUSLY WRONG PREDICTIONS

"Half of the people can be part right all of the time.
Some of the people can be all right part of the time.
But all people can't be right all of the time..."
Bob Dylan, singer/songwriter.

WISE WORDS... AND ALL THESE PEOPLE WERE TOTALLY WRONG!!!

"We don't like their sound, and guitar music is on the way out."
Decca Recording Company while rejecting The Beatles (1962).

"Computers in the future may weigh no more than 1.5 tons."
Popular Mechanics magazine (1949).

"This telephone has too many shortcomings to be seriously considered as a means of communication. The device is inherently of no value to us."
Western Union internal memo (1876).

"Heavier-than-air flying machines are impossible."
Lord Kelvin, British physicist, inventor, president of the Royal Society (1895).

"You'd better learn secretarial work or else get married."
Emmeline Snively, director, Blue Book Modelling Agency, to Norma Jean Mortenson (Marilyn Monroe).

DOH!

"People will soon get tired of staring at a plywood box every night."
Darryl F. Zanuck, on television (1946).

"A rocket will never be able to leave the Earth's atmosphere."
New York Times (1936).

"The horse is here to stay, but the automobile is only a novelty – a fad."
Michigan Savings Bank president's advice to Henry Ford's lawyer on why not to invest in Ford Motor Co.

"Airplanes are interesting toys but of no military value."
Marechal Ferdinand Foch, Professor of Strategy, Ecole Superieure de Guerre, France.

"Nuclear-powered vacuum cleaners will probably be a reality in 10 years."
Alexander Lewyt, President, Lewyt Corp (1953).

"Space travel is utter bilge."
Richard van der Riet Wooley, British Astronomer Royal (1956).

"Everything that can be invented has been invented."
Charles H. Duell, Commissioner, U.S. Office of Patents (1899).

"Rail travel at high speed is not possible because passengers, unable to breathe, would die of asphyxia."
Dr Dionysys Larder (1793–1859).

SILLY!

97

ALIENS and UFOs

Little green men from Mars? Or scary, hairy Klingons from... Klingon? Are aliens just something out of science fiction, or is there really something out there?

WHY SAUCERS?

UFOs are usually imagined as flying saucers. But why? It all started with pilot Kenneth A. Arnold, the first American to report a UFO. He was flying a plane over Washington State in 1947, when he saw nine objects that he said looked "flat like a pie-pan and somewhat bat-shaped". Newspaper articles began referring to the UFOs as flying saucers – whether it was Arnold who first used the term "flying saucers" or a reporter is still a mystery.

FACTS

Every three minutes a UFO sighting occurs somewhere on the planet.

A 1991 survey stated that four million Americans believe they have been abducted by aliens. That's as many as the population of Puerto Rico!

IF THERE ARE ALIENS, WHY WON'T THE GOVERNMENT JUST TELL US?

You may be wondering – if aliens have landed on Earth, why keep it a big secret? In 1961, NASA submitted a report called "Proposed Studies on the Implications of Peaceful Space Activities for Human Affairs". It claimed that if people were confronted with beings from another planet, we would probably freak out. Who wouldn't?

Close Encounters of the Third Kind is a classic UFO movie. But what's the third kind? Is there a first kind and a second kind? Yes.

1. A close encounter of the **first kind** is the sighting of one or more UFOs.

2. A close encounter of the **second kind** is the observation of a UFO along with physical effects like paralysis or interference on radio or TV reception.

3. A close encounter of the **third kind** is the observation of some sort of alien being alongside the spotting of a UFO.

4. A close encounter of the **fourth kind** is the serious one – abduction!

ROSWELL, 1947

The Roswell incident is the most famous UFO incident ever. On July 8, 1947 Roswell Army Air Field (RAAF) reported that they had recovered a crashed "flying disc" – then later that same day said they reported that they had actually just found a weather balloon. Mysterious? People forgot all about the incident until 1978, when Major Jesse Marcel, who had been involved with the recovery at the crash site, said they had actually found an alien spacecraft. And so, the conspiracy theory was born! The truth is out there!

RESTRICTED AREA

AREA 51

- Top-secret military base located in Nevada. It's about 128 km (80 miles) south of Las Vegas.
- The base does not appear on U.S. government maps. In fact, the government denied its very existence until 2000.
- Theorists claim that the base is used for the storage and study of alien spacecraft that have crashed to Earth, including the material found at Roswell.
- The highway that runs alongside Area 51 has been officially designated as the Extraterrestrial Highway by Nevada.

"If you look into the sky in the early morning you see them playing tag between the stars."
– Muhammad Ali

HAIR
EVERYWHERE

Some hair-raising facts about your crowning glory...

Your hair grows more quickly in warm weather than in cold.

Your hair grows faster during the day than at night.

The average lifespan of a human hair is 5 years.

By the age of 50, more than 50 per cent of men are going bald.

Your hair grows about 1.25 cm (½ inch) a month.

Hair is mostly made up of keratin, the same stuff as your fingernails.

On average, 00 hairs a day fall rom your scalp.

The longest beard on record belonged to Norwegian-born Hans Lanseth. At its longest, his beard was 5.3 m (17.5 ft) long!

QUESTIONS

You're alone in a dark room with only a gas lamp, a wood stove, and a candle. You only have one match, so what do you light first?

1

Billy's mother had four children. The first was named April, the second was named May, and the third was named June. What was the name of her fourth child?

2

How can you use the letters in NEW DOOR to make one word?

The Mississippi River is the dividing line between Arkansas and Tennessee. If an aeroplane crashed slap bang in the middle of the Mississippi River, which side would the survivors be buried?

3

Let's do some mental exercise

MIND

What can run but never walks, has a mouth but never talks, has a head but never weeps, and has a bed but never sleeps?

6

How can you cut a round cake into eight equal portions with just three straight cuts of a knife?

5

4

and give those grey cells a workout

BENDERS

Answers on p. 126...

What is lighter than a feather, yet even the strongest man in the world can't hold it for more than a few minutes?

7

If it takes five men six days to dig seven holes, how long will it take one man to dig half a hole?

8

ACTION FIGURE
Collector

The world's love affair with action figures began in 1964 when Hassenfeld Brothers (known today as Hasbro) unveiled a line of 30 cm (12 in), fully articulated *G.I. Joe* Action Soldiers. They were basically Barbie dolls for boys, and came complete with vehicles and accessories. Then in 1977, the action figure industry changed with the release of a movie called *Star Wars*. Toy company Kenner released smaller 9.5 cm (3¾ in) figures, which were so popular they became the new standard.

KNOW YOUR ACTION-FIGURE LINGO!

Articulation – The movable parts and joints on an action figure.

Die-cast – A metal or plastic toy made in a die or mould.

Blister pack – The clear (and often frustratingly difficult to open) clear plastic shell that encases the action figure and its accessories.

MOC – Mint on card, basically the figure is unopened. What a shame!

Loose – Any toy that's no longer in its original packaging.

Shortpack – Action figures that are deliberately produced in small numbers to create a high level of demand. Shortpack figures are the ones collectors want most.

The most expensive action figure ever

Nothing beats an original. Created by Don Levine, the prototype for the original 1963 G.I. Joe sold to collector Steve Geppi for £120,000 in 2003!

Tantalizing toy fact

During the 1978 holiday season, Kenner sold more than 42 million *Star Wars* action figures!

THE RATING GAME

The quality and condition of boxed action figures is rated on something called the "C" scale.

C10: Perfect and incredibly rare.

C9: Very few defects. Excellent collector-quality toys.

C8.5: Very good condition, but collectors may avoid them.

C8: Visible flaws. The lowest collector-grade rating.

C6/7: Apparent flaws. Not for collectors – just for fun.

C5 and lower: Very poor quality. Well-worn with many parts missing.

BE AN ACTION FIGURE

Collecting *Star Wars* and other action figures is cool enough, but what if *you* were the action figure? Today, it's possible. There are plenty of companies on the Internet who will sculpt a custom action figure of you. You can even add stuff like speech capability, custom clothes, tattoos, and crazy accessories. You just need to provide a photo.

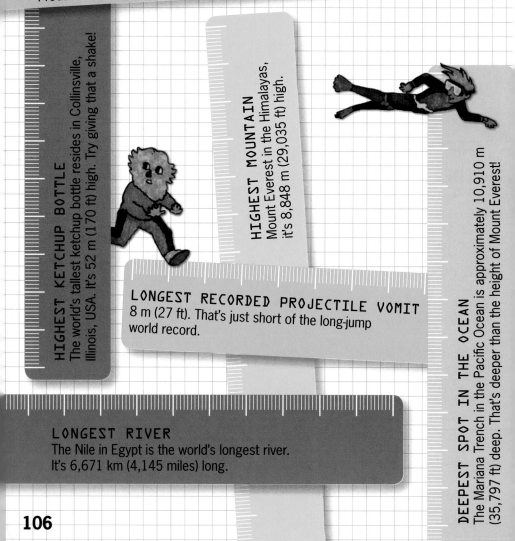

LONGEST HOT DOG
In 1996, Sara Lee made the world's longest hot dog at 608 m (1,996 ft) – but they didn't have a continuous bun, so sorry no record! The record belongs to Shizuoka Meat Producers of Japan, who made a 600 m (1,969 ft) long frankfurter in a bun in 2006.

HIGHEST KETCHUP BOTTLE
The world's tallest ketchup bottle resides in Collinsville, Illinois, USA. It's 52 m (170 ft) high. Try giving that a shake!

HIGHEST MOUNTAIN
Mount Everest in the Himalayas, it's 8,848 m (29,035 ft) high.

LONGEST RECORDED PROJECTILE VOMIT
8 m (27 ft). That's just short of the long-jump world record.

DEEPEST SPOT IN THE OCEAN
The Mariana Trench in the Pacific Ocean is approximately 10,910 m (35,797 ft) deep. That's deeper than the height of Mount Everest!

LONGEST RIVER
The Nile in Egypt is the world's longest river. It's 6,671 km (4,145 miles) long.

DEEPEST, HIGHEST

SHORTEST ESCALATOR
Located in Kawasaki More's department store in Japan, the world's shortest escalator is only 8.43 cm (3⅓ in) high!

HIGHEST HOUSE OF CARDS
Card stacker Bryan Berg set the world record for the highest house of cards with a monstrous 7.7 m (25 ft 3.5 in) card mansion. It took 2,400 decks to build it. Well it's cheaper than bricks and mortar!

LONGEST CONGA LINE
On March 13, 1998, in Miami, 119,986 people joined together in one gigantic conga line, setting the world record.

SHORTEST RIVER
According to the *Guinness Book of World Records*, the Roe River in Great Falls, USA, is the world's tiniest. It's only 60 m (200 ft) long.

HIGHEST WATERFALL
Angel Falls in Canaima National Park, Venezuela is the highest waterfall in the world at 980 m (3,212 ft).

LONGEST CAR
Jay Ohrberg designed the world's longest car – a 30 m (100 ft) limo that has 26 wheels. It even has two steering wheels, one at each end to help it back up! It comes equipped with a Jacuzzi, helipad, sundeck, and swimming pool (including diving board!).

WEIRD

In Canada, you can't pay for a fifty-cent item with only pennies.

In England, it's illegal to hang a bed out of a window.

In France, it's against the law to die unless you've already purchased a cemetery plot.

In Mexico, you can't lift either foot off the pedals while riding a bicycle, because you might lose control.

LAWS

In Switzerland, it's against the law to flush the toilet after 10 o'clock at night.

In Thailand, it's illegal to leave your house if you're not wearing underwear.

In Australia, you can't wear hot-pink trousers past 4 o'clock on a Sunday.

In Israel, it's against the law to bring a bear to the beach.

In Australia, taxi cabs must carry a bale of hay in their boot at all times.

BIGFEET, YETIS, SASQUATCHES, AND SNOWMEN

Bigfoot, also known as Sasquatch, is a large ape-like creature that supposedly prowls the Pacific Northwest region of North America. No hard evidence has ever been found that proves the existence of such a creature. In 1967, two men claimed to have captured footage of Bigfoot in California. Their short film clip is the best evidence that Bigfoot exists. But the recording is grainy and many people claim it's a hoax. Other similar creatures are said to inhabit other parts of the world. For example, the Yeti (also known as the Abominable Snowman), roams the Himalayan region of Nepal.

MYSTERIOUS
MYSTE

SOME THINGS IN LIFE CAN'T BE EXPLAINED... BUT HERE ARE A FEW FAMOUS MYSTERIES THAT HAVE

MISSING PLANES AND BOATS

The Bermuda Triangle (also known as the Devil's Triangle), is a section of the Atlantic Ocean between Florida, Bermuda, and San Juan in Puerto Rico. A vast number of planes and boats have gone missing in this area with no explanation at all. Some people claim it's haunted, others suspect that aliens have visited the spot, while others put it down to a time-travel portal.

The most infamous Bermuda Triangle incident is the story of the USS *Cyclops*. In 1918, the ship and its entire crew of 309 went missing in the Bermuda Triangle. They were never found.

A MUMMY'S CURSE?

King Tut's tomb is one of the most fascinating discoveries of our time. But could there be a curse surrounding it? The mystery began just weeks after the opening of the tomb when Lord Carnarvon, the man who funded the exploration, died. It was said that all the lights of Cairo went out the instant he passed away.

Speculation only increased when it was revealed that inside the tomb an inscription was found on a shrine to Anubis, the god of the dead, which read "It is I who hinder the sand from choking the secret chamber. I am for the protection of the deceased."

RIES

THEY DO MAKE GREAT STORIES. PERPLEXED HUMANKIND.

Years after, newspapers continued to report the deaths of those related to the discovery of the tomb. So could there really be a curse?

A MISSING CIVILIZATION?

Atlantis is a legendary island that was first mentioned in the writings of the Greek philosopher Plato. In his account, Atlantis was a beautiful island society that prospered around 9600 BCE. But after its people tried to invade Athens, the island sank into the ocean and was never seen again. Dozens of possible locations for Atlantis have been suggested, including Santorini in Greece, the Azores in the Atlantic, and off the coast of Cornwall in England.

ANCIENT EGYPT

The story of ancient Egypt

5,000 years ago farmers first began to settle along the Nile River. After a time, two separate kingdoms developed – Upper Egypt and Lower Egypt. In 3200 BCE the pharaoh of Upper Egypt conquered Lower Egypt and the kingdom was united. This was the true beginning of ancient Egypt. The society prospered for the next 3,000 years until they were conquered by the Romans in 31 BCE.

King Tut's tomb

In 1922, British archaeologist Howard Carter discovered Tutankhamun's (King Tut's) tomb. It was almost perfectly preserved, and full of treasure, including a solid gold mask of the king's face. Today, King Tut is one of the most famous of all the ancient Egyptian pharaohs, but he was actually quite an unimportant ruler. He became pharaoh when he was only 9 and died when he was just 18.

The Nile life

Most ancient Egyptians were farmers. They lived in mud-brick houses, which kept them cool under the hot Egyptian sun. Every year the Nile would flood and the farmers would plant their crops in the fertile flood banks.

⚠ The ancient Egyptians believed fried mice would cure a toothache.

⚠ Pharaohs never let their hair be seen – they would always wear a headdress.

⚠ The ancient Egyptians invented makeup!

By the gods!

The ancient Egyptians worshipped over 2,000 gods! Their gods and goddesses were often represented by a human with the head of an animal. One of the most famous Egyptian gods was Ra, the Sun god. He wore a mask of a falcon, with a sun disc balanced on top.

Mummies

When you think of Egypt, you probably think of mummies. A mummy is a body that has been preserved after death. The ancient Egyptians mummified human bodies because they believed it would help them to have a safe voyage into the afterlife. Because mummification was expensive, the richer someone was, the better mummified they would be and the more complex their burial. A well-mummified body would be preserved for much longer.

The pyramids

The pyramids were giant tombs built for the pharaohs. The three pyramids of Giza, near Cairo, are still standing and Khufu's pyramid, the largest of the three, is considered one of the seven wonders of the ancient world. In fact, Khufu's pyramid, also known as the Great Pyramid of Giza, was the tallest building in the world for 5,000 years until the Eiffel Tower was built in 1889.

EWW! Disgusting facts about gruesome things

A selection of squishy, slimy, and utterly disgusting facts about really gross things.

On average, people swallow 14 insects a year while they sleep! Talk about a midnight feast… yuk!

65 per cent of nose pickers use their index finger.

A cockroach can live for nine days without its head.

You swallow about one litre (two pints) of mucus and snot every day. Yum.

Many popular brands of yogurt and jelly contain pork gelatin. We're all for sausage-flavoured yogurt – aren't we?

A 450g (1 lb) jar of peanut butter can contain up to five rodent hairs and 150 bug fragments. Maybe spread something different on your next sandwich?

In ancient Rome, when men took part in the Olympic games, they did it entirely naked.

A single pair of rats can produce 15,000 descendents in a year – and 20 million in three years.

Parasites count for 0.01 per cent of your body weight.

The average person's bed is home to more than 6 billion dust mites. Imagine sharing a duvet with that lot!

People fart an average of **14 TIMES** a day.

The world record for eating live maggots is 100 in less than 5½ minutes.

TWIN-TUITION? Could twins actually have extra sensory perception (ESP)? Well, no one seems to know for sure. Science says no. But there are countless sets of twins who claim they share some sort of paranormal connection. The most common examples of "twin-tuition" are things like finishing each other's sentences, knowing what the other twin is thinking, and even feeling each other's pain.

THE JIM TWINS: There are many cases of twins being separated at birth, only to meet years later and discover how similar they are. The most extreme example is the "Jim Twins". Jim Lewis and Jim Springer were adopted by separate families when they were just one month old. They reunited when they were 39 and they couldn't believe the amazing things they had in common...

• They had both been married twice – both first wives were named Linda and both second wives were named Betty.
• One Jim named his son James Allan – the other named his son James Alan.
• They had both been employed as sheriffs, and both bit their fingernails.

IDENTICAL TWINS have virtually the same DNA – but not the same fingerprints. So if you have an identical twin, you can't frame them for stealing the biscuits for your midnight feast!

The fancy science word for identical twins is **MONOZYGOTIC**.
Fraternal twins are called **DIZYGOTIC**.

ELVIS PRESLEY WAS A TWIN but his sibling died at birth.

MOST TWINS ARE BORN ON THE SAME DAY but they don't have to be! The longest gap between twin birth dates is 85 days.

TWINS OCCUR IN OTHER SPECIES APART FROM HUMANS, most commonly in cats, sheep, deer, and ferrets. In fact, one species of armadillo has litters of identical quadruplets as its normal method of reproduction.

Best things ever said about POLITICS

"Before I refuse to take your questions, I have an opening statement."

Ronald Reagan, US President (1981–89)

"You're working hard to put food on your family."

George W. Bush, US President (2001–09)

"Politics, it seems to me, for years, or all too long, has been concerned with right or left instead of right or wrong."

Richard Armour, poet

"Democracy is being allowed to vote for the candidate you dislike least."

Robert Byrne, author

"Solutions are not the answer."

Richard Nixon, US President (1969–74)

"Politics, n: [Poly "many" + tics "blood-sucking parasites"]"

Larry Hardiman

"Any American who is prepared to run for president should automatically, by definition, be disqualified from ever doing so."

Gore Vidal, author

"Whenever I hear anyone arguing for slavery, I feel a strong impulse to see it tried on him personally."

Abraham Lincoln,
US President (1861–65)

"I have come to the conclusion that politics is too serious a matter to be left to the politicians."

Charles de Gaulle,
President of France (1959–69)

"If you haven't found something worth dying for, you aren't fit to be living."

Martin Luther King, Jr.

"Ask not what your country can do for you; ask what you can do for your country."

John Fitzgerald Kennedy,
US President (1961–63)

"Being powerful is like being a lady. If you have to tell people you are, you aren't."

Margaret Thatcher, British Prime Minister (1979–90)

MEGAWORDS

Want to impress your friends with really, really, really, really, really long words? You'd better know what they mean first. Here's a long list!

Hippopotomonstrosesquipediliophobia

Some wordsmith out there has a good sense of humour. This super-long word means "the fear of long words".

Misodoctakleidist

Someone who hates playing the piano.

Squirrelled

Longest one-syllable word.

Floccinaucinihilipilification

This was the longest word to appear in the first edition of the Oxford English Dictionary. It's defined as "the action or habit of estimating as worthless".

Honorificabilitudinitatibus

In 1721, this was recognized as the longest word in the English language. It's just a really, really long way of saying "honourableness" or "having honour."

Humuhumunukunukuapua'a

A Hawaiian fish. It's been said that the name is longer than the fish.

Chargoggagoggmanchauggagoggchaubunagungamaugg

This monster name refers to a lake in Massachusetts, USA. It's literally translated as, "I'll fish on the right side, you fish on the left side, no one fishes in the middle."

Trichophagia

The extremely unhealthy habit of eating lots of hair.

Twyndyllyngs

This is the longest English word without any of the five vowels. It means twins.

BUILD A

BUILD YOUR OWN →

EVER WONDERED HOW GREAT IT WOULD BE TO DISCOVER BURIED TREASURE? WHY NOT MAKE YOUR OWN?

HOW LONG?

First step: decide how long you want it to remain unopened for. You can go for one year, 10, or even 50 years, and see how much things have changed. Or you could leave if for 500 years, ready to be discovered by an alien leader.

THE CAPSULE

The container you use to create the capsule will depend on where you put it. To bury or not to bury? That is the question. If you want to dig a hole, find a box that won't rot or decay in the ground – it has to be waterproof.

ALMOST DONE

Okay, almost finished. On the front, write in big bold letters, "DO NOT OPEN UNTIL," and a date. Then bury or hide it, and forget about it. But not totally, otherwise you'll forget to find it.

WHAT TO INCLUDE

It's up to you, but here are a few suggestions:
• Magazine clippings
• Photos of you and your family
• A letter to your future self
• Popular toys
• Labels from your favourite foods
Put each item in an individual bag.

WHAT NOT TO INCLUDE

• Food of any sort. As tempted as you may be to see what a banana looks like 10 years from now, don't do it!
• Any liquid that isn't sealed tight.
• Anything with a strong odour (especially if you're going to bury it – you'll attract all the dogs in the neighbourhood!)

IT MAKES YOU FEEL LIKE A PIRATE FROM THE MOVIES, HIDING YOUR TREASURE

A **time capsule** is anything that saves stuff with the intention of being found and opened at a later time. The modern idea of a planned time capsule has been around since the 1930s.

TIME CAPSULE

TIME CAPSULE FACTS!

Register that bad boy! If you want to be official, register your time capsule. You can write to the **International Time Capsule Society** at: International Time Capsule Society, Oglethorpe University, 4484 Peachtree Road NE, Atlanta, GA 30319-2797, USA.

The International Time Capsule Society keeps a database of every registered time capsule on the planet.

BURYING YOUR TIME CAPSULE CAN BE PROBLEMATIC! Need proof? The town of Corona, California has lost track of 17 different buried time capsules.

The Crypt of Civilization at Oglethorpe University in Atlanta, USA, is generally considered to be THE FIRST SUCCESSFUL, ORGANIZED BURIED TIME CAPSULE. It was built in 1936 and isn't scheduled to be opened for THOUSANDS of years – not until 8113 to be exact. Inside is a Bible, a machine to teach the English language, and last but not least, SOME BUDWEISER BEER.

The phrase "time capsule" was first coined in 1937. Originally, it was going to be called a "time bomb". Then someone realized that was a little scary, and changed it to time capsule. (If you discovered something in the ground with the words TIME BOMB written across it, would you really want to open it?)

There are 1,400 time capsule groups registered worldwide and those groups estimate that there are nearly 15,000 time capsules spread across the world. Sadly, they think 80% of all time capsules are forgotten about.

PRIVATE: DO NOT OPEN

APRIL FOOLS' FOOLS

APRIL 1ST. What a day! Pranks and jokes abound. Here are a few classics from April Fools' Days past...

Bombs Away!

It was 1915, the middle of World War 1, when a French pilot flew over a German camp and dropped what looked like a giant bomb. The German soldiers thought they were done for. But there was no explosion. They approached the bomb and discovered it was actually a football, with a note attached that read "April Fool!"

Big Digital Ben

On April 1st, 1980, the BBC reported that the most famous clock in the world, London's Big Ben, would be switching to a digital readout in order to keep up with the times. People were furious, until the BBC let them in on the joke.

Incoming Wasps!

In 1949, a New Zealand radio DJ announced that a mile-wide swarm of wasps was heading for Auckland. He urged everyone to leave honey traps outside their homes and to wear their socks over their trousers, so that no flesh was exposed. The New Zealand Broadcasting Service didn't think the joke was funny and to this day a warning memo is sent out every year before April Fool's Day.

Lefty Burger
In 1998, Burger King ran an advert in USA Today announcing the brand new Left-Handed Whopper – a burger with the ketchup, cheese, and all the other condiments switched 180 degrees for left-handed burger eaters. Thousands of customers ran to Burger King requesting lefty burgers.

White Doggies
In 1965 a Copenhagen newspaper reported that the Danish parliament had passed a bizarre new law requiring all dogs to be painted white so they would be seen more easily at night. Whether or not anyone actually painted their dog white – well, we can only imagine.

The Swiss Spaghetti Harvest
In 1957, the BBC news programme *Panorama* proclaimed that, thanks to the "virtual disappearance of the spaghetti weevil", the year's Swiss spaghetti crop would be bigger than ever. A video clip showed Swiss farmers pulling spaghetti from trees. People believed it! Viewers called in, asking how to grow their own. The BBC responded, "Place a sprig of spaghetti in a tin of tomato sauce and hope for the best".

Look Ma, No Gravity!
In 1976, famous astronomer Patrick Moore went on BBC Radio and announced that a once-in-a-lifetime astronomical event was about to occur. Pluto was going to pass behind Jupiter, causing a gravitational shift that would briefly reduce Earth's own gravity. Moore told listeners that if they jumped at the exact moment it occurred, they'd be able to float in the air for a moment. Hundreds of people tried it – some even called the BBC, saying it worked!

ANSWERS

P27 Wonders of the World

Great Pyramid of Giza
Hanging Gardens of Babylon
Temple of Artemis at Ephesus
Statue of Zeus at Olympia
Mausoleum of Maussollos at Halicarnassus
Colossus of Rhodes
Lighthouse of Alexandria

P24 – 25 Who Am I?

WHO? Walt Disney
WHERE? Eiffel Tower
WHAT? Typewriter

P28 – 29 Brainteasers

1. Just one, then it isn't empty anymore.
2. He escaped in the winter, when the water surrounding the island had frozen. He walked across the ice.
3. They weren't playing against each other.
4. The man was bald.
5. Short (shorter).
6. 31,536,000 (or in a leap year - 31,622,400.)
7. They were a grandfather, father, and son.

P60 Scaly!

Antarctica. It's too cold.

P62 Phobias

- Telephonophobia – Fear of telephones
- Amnesiphobia – Fear of amnesia
- Nudophobia – Fear of nudity
- Somniphobia – Fear of sleep
- Carnophobia – Fear of meat
- Bibliophobia – Fear of books

126

P102 – 103 Mindbenders

1. The match!
2. The fourth child was called Billy.
3. Nowhere – you don't bury survivors!
4. "one word" is an anagram of "new door".
5. Cut the cake into quarters (that's two cuts) and then stack the quarters on top of one another, and then cut that stack in half.
6. A river.
7. Your breath!
8. There's no such thing as "half a hole". A hole is a hole, doesn't matter how big or small.

WOW!

Cool!

DID YOU KNOW?
THE BRAIN IS
EXTREMELY FAST!
IT SENDS MESSAGES
ALONG ITS NEURONS
AT SPEEDS OF
365 KM/H (225 MPH).

ACKNOWLEDGEMENTS

Max Brallier would like to thank Abby, for putting up with him. With love.

Dorling Kindersley would like to thank Fleur Star for her editorial help; and Clemence Monot, Emma Forge, and Tom Forge for their design assistance.

The publisher would like to thank the following for their kind permission to reproduce their photographs:

(Key: a-above; b-below/bottom; c-centre; f-far; l-left; r-right; t-top)

Alamy Images: Andy Ennis 105tr; Mary Evans Picture Library 8cr; National Motor Museum / Motoring Picture Library 18br; PhotoStock-Israel 104bl. **Walt Anthony:** 70cr. **Corbis:** Danny Lehman 54-55 (background); Louie Psihoyos 19tr. **DK Images:** Robert L. Braun - modelmaker 10cb, 10ftr; The British Museum 112-113; Centaur Studios - modelmakers 10-11c; Coca Cola 8fclb; Graham High at Centaur Studios - modelmaker 11ca; Sean Hunter 55bl; Imperial War Museum, Duxford 9ftr; London Planetarium 76fcr; Jamie Marshall 55fcla; Judith Miller / Cooper Owen 9clb; Judith Miller / Noel Barrett Antiques & Auctions Ltd 9tc; NASA 76fcrb, 98tl; NASA / Finley Holiday Films 77fbr, 99c; Stephen Oliver 34cr, 34crb, 34fbl, 34fcl, 34fcr, 35fbr, 55br; Luis Rey - modelmaker 10cl; Rough Guides 54fbr, 54fcl, 55cla; Royal Tyrrell Museum of Palaeontology, Alberta, Canada 11bl; Jerry Young 18bl. **FLPA:** Steven Ruiter / FN / Minden 19crb. **Getty Images:** De Agostini Picture Library / DEA / W. Buss 54clb; fStop / Halfdark 36tl, 37br; Ciaran Griffin / Stockbyte 18tc; Iconica / Arctic-Images 10-11 (background); Illustration Works / Dietrich Madsen 56-57b; The Image Bank / Ed Freeman 54crb; Photographer's Choice / Chris Collins 94-95 (border); Andy Rouse / The Image Bank 19br; Stockbyte / John Foxx 94-95 (background); Stocktrek RF 78fbl, 79cl, 79fbr, 79tr; Taxi / James Porto 78-79; Visuals Unlimited / Ken Lucas 11br; Toru Yamanaka / AFP 18cla. **iStockphoto.com:**

Mads Abildgaard 28-29; Apatrimonio 44-45c; Arlindo71 88fclb (ant); Mike Bentley 32-33 (background); Matjaz Boncina 36-37 (background); James Bowyer 60cb, 61clb, 61tr; Jens Carsten 70bl; CostinT 66-67; Cyfrogclone 42-43 (background / soda cup); Julie de Leseleuc 44cl, 44clb, 45fbr, 45ftr; David Dea 52bl; Hywit Dimyadi 125tc; Gabriela Durán 44c; Hannah Eckman 40clb; Jamie Farrant 110-111; Julie Felton 102c (brain), 102ca (brain), 102cra (brain), 102fbl (brain), 103br (brain), 103cla (brain), 103fbr (brain), 103fcl (brain), 103fcrb (brain), 103tr (brain); Graffizone 118bc, 118bl, 118-119b; KarlKotas Inc. 32cra; KateLeigh 72bl, 73br, 73fcla; Attila Kis 71tl; Sergey Krivoruchko 71bl; Abel Leão 114-115; Liangpv 108-109tc; Bill Noll 22-23 (background); Skip O'Donnell 28fclb, 29tl; Kirsty Pargeter 46-47; Pavlen 92tl; Plainview 58-59 (background); RTimages 3c; RussellTatedotCom 104-105 (background); Anssi Ruuska 109ftr; Saw 40tl, 68-69 (background); Scibak 108ftl (window); Chris Scredon 64 (background), 65 (background); Simon2579 118-119 (background); Dieter Spears 118-119c; Song Speckels 44tc; SpiffyJ 71cr; Mark Stay 102c (legs), 102ca (legs), 102cra (legs), 102fbl (legs), 103br (legs), 103cla (legs), 103fbr (legs), 103fcl (legs), 103fcrb (legs), 103tr (legs); Stocksnapper 1cb; Tornograf 93tr; Hans Van Ijzendoorn 93cra; Kristina Velickovic 42-43 (background / ice creams); Graça Victoria 88fclb (cake); Klara Viskova 46fbl, 47fbr; John Woodcock 48c, 48tl; Serdar Yagci 60-61 (background); Robertas Pižas 88-89 (background). **National Geographic Stock:** Stephen Alvarez 76-77 (background). **Rex Features:** South West News Service 19cra. **Science Photo Library:** Robert Gendler 98-99 (background); Nancy Kedersha 126-127 (background); Pasieka 127cb.

All other images © Dorling Kindersley
For further information see:
www.dkimages.com